T0370198

SPIRITUALITY
+
RECOVERY

A Practical Guide
to SPIRITUAL CONCEPTS, PRINCIPLES
and PRACTICES used in RECOVERY
and the 12 Steps

- WHAT THEY MEAN
- HOW THEY WORK
- WAYS TO USE THEM

Susan Chance, M.A.

ISBN 979-8-35095-822-5 (soft cover)
ISBN 979-8-35098-388-3 (hard cover)

AUTHOR'S NOTE

In the intricate tapestry of life, addiction emerges as a dark thread, weaving its way through the fabric of existence, obscuring the vibrant hues of love, connection, and joy that are our birthright. My journey into the heart of this darkness is not unique, yet it is deeply personal. The cost of addiction is immeasurable, silently dissolving the bonds of friendship, family, and community, undermining health, aspirations, and the very core of our being. It's a path that leads to a profound disconnection from our true selves, marked by a dwindling spiral of self-will, trust, esteem, and respect. This journey into shadow is fraught with isolation, shame, and a profound sense of loss.

My own awakening from this nightmare began in the depths of despair, at a moment when everything that had once given my life meaning seemed irrevocably lost. Faced with the stark reality of my situation—on the brink of death or imprisonment—I realized the necessity of facing my demons head-on. It was this epiphany that kindled a spark of determination within me—a resolve to reclaim my life from the clutches of addiction.

Embarking on this path of recovery, I committed myself whole-heartedly to the process, traversing the new challenges of rehabilitation, sober living environments, and the transformative power of Twelve-Step programs. My experience as a Twelve Step peer and sponsor further deepened my understanding of the recovery journey. Yet, it was the elusive promise of spirituality that beckoned me with its vow of deeper healing. My quest for spiritual understanding propelled me into a voracious exploration of self-help, addiction recovery, and spiritual wisdom, culminating in a master's degree in Spiritual Psychology and certification as a Meditation Instructor.

This journey was not merely academic; it was a pilgrimage of the soul, seeking to integrate spiritual principles and practices into the very fabric of my daily existence. The adoption of these practices into my life laid the cornerstone for a newfound stability within myself, a sanctuary from which I could weather the storms of recovery and life. This spiritual foundation has been transformative, enabling me to shed destructive habits, cultivate self-awareness and resilience, and live a life of authenticity and purpose.

This book is born out of my journey and the lessons I learned along the way. It is a guiding hand for those navigating the murky waters of addiction and recovery, offering clarity, inspiration, and practical guidance. It is my deepest hope that within these pages, you will find the tools and wisdom to build your own foundation of strength and stability, lighting your path towards a life of wellness and profound fulfillment. May this guide serve as a loyal companion on your journey to reclaiming your life, offering a beacon of hope and transformation.

INTRODUCTION

In the profound journey of recovery and wellness, the integration of spirituality emerges not merely as an aid but as a cornerstone of healing and transformation. *Spirituality + Recovery: A Practical Guide to Spiritual Concepts, Principles and Practices used in Recovery and the Twelve Steps* is an essential companion for those navigating the complexities of healing, offering a rich entwining of spiritual wisdom and practical means to guide the way. This book is crafted to serve not just as a manual but as a source of inspiration, illuminating the path towards a life of resilience, fulfillment, and profound personal growth.

At the heart of this guide lies the acknowledgment that recovery transcends the mere cessation of addictive behaviors; it is about embarking on a transformative journey towards wellness, rediscovering one's authentic self, and nurturing the spirit. The book unfolds as a comprehensive exploration of spiritual concepts, principles, and practices, presenting them not as abstract ideals but as tangible, accessible tools for life transformation. It demystifies spirituality, making it relatable and relevant to individuals from all walks of life, regardless of their spiritual or religious backgrounds.

Spirituality + Recovery: A Practical Guide to Spiritual Concepts, Principles and Practices used in Recovery and the Twelve Steps delves into the essence of foundational spiritual concepts such as the mind-body-soul connection, unity, higher power, and self-awareness, presenting them in a manner that is easy to grasp and apply. It explores spiritual principles ranging from acceptance to faith, hope, and courage, offering them as pillars upon which to build a resilient, fulfilling life. The guide also introduces practical strategies for incorporating spiritual practices into the recovery process, including meditation, mindfulness, nature, sacred rituals, creative expression, and engagement with nature, alongside innovative healing applications like reframing, self-love, and re-parenting.

Structured to serve as a steadfast companion on your journey, the book is replete with spiritual meaning, tangible benefits, and actionable ways to incorporate what calls to you, encouraging you to explore and embrace the spiritual facets of your own recovery journey. Whether you are taking your first steps towards recovery, seeking to deepen your spiritual journey, or supporting someone on theirs, this guide offers the knowledge, inspiration, and practical steps to harness the healing power of spiritual principles and practices.

Spirituality + Recovery: A Practical Guide to Spiritual Concepts, Principles and Practices used in Recovery and the Twelve Steps invites you on a transformative journey, one where the worlds of spirituality and recovery intertwine to foster a life of wellness, purpose, and boundless potential. It stands as a testament to the transformative power of spirituality, offering a flexible toolkit for those ready to navigate the challenges of recovery with grace, perseverance, and a deepened sense of interconnectedness with the larger web of life. Welcome to a journey of self-discovery, healing, and profound personal growth, where each page brings you closer to rediscovering your inner sanctuary of peace, strength, and wisdom.

TABLE OF CONTENTS

INTRODUCTION..vii

RECOVERY...1

SPIRITUALITY...3

SPIRITUALITY VS. RELIGION......................................7

RECOVERY AND THE SPIRITUAL JOURNEY................11

SPIRITUAL CONCEPTS, PRINCIPLES, AND PRACTICES.......13

SPIRITUAL CONCEPTS

SPIRITUAL AWAKENING VS. ENLIGHTENMENT.............................. 15
SELF-REALIZATION..17
EGO AND FALSE PRIDE 21
HIGHER SELF...27
HIGHER POWER..31
DIVINE INTERVENTION 39
UNITY 43
MIND-BODY-SOUL CONNECTION...47

SPIRITUAL PRINCIPLES

HONESTY 53
HUMILITY..59
HOPE...63
COURAGE...67
FAITH..71
FORGIVENESS...75

GRATITUDE...79

COMPASSION 83

ACCEPTANCE..89

SURRENDER..93

WILLINGNESS..97

INTEGRITY..101

SPIRITUAL PRACTICES

PRAYER..105

MEDITATION 109

MINDFULNESS 113

SELF-LOVE...117

CONTEMPLATION 121

SACRED RITUALS..125

SELF-CARE...129

JOURNALING 133

SERVICE...137

COMMUNITY 141

NATURE..145

SACRED READING...149

MINDFUL MOVEMENT..153

SPIRITUAL HEALING APPLICATIONS

INNER CHILD 157

SELF-PARENTING...161

REFRAMING..165

"If we are facing in the right direction, all we have to do is keep on walking." — Zen Proverb

RECOVERY

What is recovery?

Recovery is often associated with substance abuse such as drug or alcohol addiction, but it also expands its reach to encompass other destructive behaviors such as gambling, compulsive eating, co-dependency, sex addiction, or self-harm. It is a comprehensive and ongoing effort that goes beyond mere abstinence from addictive substances or behaviors. Recovery involves addressing the underlying issues, developing coping strategies, and committing to positive changes that promote a healthier and more fulfilling life.

The journey of recovery extends beyond breaking free from the chains of addiction. It becomes a profound personal quest for self-improvement and healing, encompassing various dimensions of well-being: physical, psychological, social, spiritual, and emotional. This transformative process aims to achieve and maintain sobriety while nurturing an overall sense of wellness. Recovery represents a dynamic progression of growth, restoration, and renewal, one where we transition from a challenging or compromised state to one that is more desirable and functional.

At its core, recovery serves as a beacon of hope, guiding us toward a brighter future. It is grounded in the belief that every person possesses unique strengths and abilities. By harnessing and nurturing these inherent capabilities, we can strengthen our resilience and facilitate progress along our path of recovery. This shift in focus empowers us to recognize and foster our innate potential rather than dwelling on weaknesses or failures, enabling us to thrive despite adversity.

Within the realm of recovery, there is a profound recognition of the interconnectedness between the various aspects of an individual's life. The journey does not unfold in isolation; rather, it intertwines within the complex interaction of personal relationships, social contexts, and environmental factors. This realization necessitates a holistic approach that considers the multidimensional aspects of one's existence. Each piece contributes to the totality of the recovery story, underscoring the importance of addressing all dimensions of life to foster sustained healing and growth.

Furthermore, the concept of recovery embodies the truth that no two journeys are identical. Each person's path to a healthy self is unique; it is shaped by their individual experiences, strengths, and aspirations. While recovery may involve shared experiences and the collective wisdom of support groups or therapy, it is ultimately a deeply personal voyage. It is tailored to fit the specific needs, beliefs, and values of each person, honoring their individuality and empowering them to find their own authentic path to recovery.

"All that is true, by whomsoever it has been said has its origin in the Spirit." — Thomas Aquinas

SPIRITUALITY

What is spirituality?

In its broadest sense, the term spirituality is a name given to matters of the spirit. These can be any kind of meaningful personal activities or peaceful experiences. It is a concept, so people can see and understand it in different ways. The term spirit itself means "animating or vital principle in man and animals." It is derived from the Old French word *espirit*, which comes from the Latin word *spiritus* (soul, ghost, courage, vigor, breath) and is related to *spirare* (the Latin word to -breathe).

The origins of spirituality is a topic that has fascinated and intrigued humanity for centuries. The concept of spirituality can be traced back to the dawn of human civilizations, as our ancestors began to seek a deeper understanding of the world around them. Over time, spirituality has evolved and taken on diverse forms, influenced by various cultures and belief systems.

In ancient times, primitive humans embarked on a quest and began to comprehend the mysteries of life, death, and the natural world. They sought to make sense of their place in the vast universe, contemplating the forces that govern it and pondering the existence of realms beyond the physical.

Among tribal societies, spirituality emerged as a means of connecting with the divine or supernatural realms. Shamans, medicine men and women, and tribal elders played vital roles as intermediaries between the physical and spiritual worlds, providing guidance and healing as well as conducting rituals that were believed to bridge the gap between the human and spiritual realms, fostering a sense of unity and harmony within the community.

As civilizations developed and organized religions emerged, spirituality became intertwined with cultural, societal, and moral frameworks. Early civilizations like the Egyptians, Mesopotamians, Greeks, and Romans worshipped pantheons of gods and goddesses. Religious rituals were conducted to establish a connection with the divine, seek blessings, and navigate the complexities of life.

In ancient Eastern cultures such as India and China, spirituality was explored through philosophies like Hinduism, Buddhism, Taoism, and Confucianism. These belief systems focused on inner transformation, self-realization, and the pursuit of enlightenment or spiritual awakening. They emphasized the development of moral virtues, meditation practices, and self-discipline to attain a deeper understanding of the self and the universe.

Throughout history, mystical and esoteric traditions emerged within the context of various religious and spiritual quests. Individuals seeking direct personal experiences of the divine embarked on these paths, engaging in practices such as meditation, contemplation, prayer, and rituals. These practices aimed to transcend the material world and establish a profound connection with the spiritual realm, cultivating spiritual growth and awakening.

It is important to recognize that spirituality is a deeply subjective and personal experience. While there are common themes and practices that exist across different cultures and belief systems, the expression and interpretation of spirituality can vary widely from person to person. Each individual brings their own unique perspectives, beliefs, and experiences to their spiritual journey.

Spirituality is a complex foundation stone of human history. It reflects our innate curiosity—our search for meaning, purpose, and connection with the divine. From tribal practices to organized religions and philosophical systems, spirituality continues to evolve and shape our understanding of ourselves, the world, and our place in it.

> *"Religion is a map, spirituality is a journey."*
> — Steve Jobs

SPIRITUALITY VS. RELIGION

What are the differences between spirituality and religion?

Spirituality and religion are related concepts, but they have distinct differences in their focus, practices, beliefs, and approaches. Here are some key differentiations between spirituality and religion:

Nature of Beliefs:

- **Spirituality:** Spirituality often focuses on personal and individual views, experiences, and connections to the divine or higher power. It can encompass a wide range of beliefs and practices that may or may not align with organized religious doctrines.

- **Religion:** Religion typically involves adherence to a specific set of beliefs, teachings, rituals, and practices that are codified within a religious tradition. It often includes a defined theology, organized rituals, and a hierarchical structure.

Institutional Structure:

- **Spirituality:** Spirituality is often more individualistic and can be practiced outside of formal institutions. It emphasizes a personal relationship with the divine or higher power, and we may follow our own unique paths.

- **Religion:** Religion is organized into established institutions with defined leadership, hierarchies, and specific doctrines. It often involves membership in a religious community or organization.

Rituals and Practices:

- **Spirituality:** Spiritual practices can vary widely and are often tailored to an individual's beliefs and needs. Practices may include meditation, mindfulness, contemplation, service, and other activities that promote inner growth and connection.

- **Religion:** Religious practices are often standardized and prescribed by the religious tradition. They may include regular attendance at religious services, specific prayers, rituals, sacraments, and other ceremonies.

Approach to Dogma:

- **Spirituality:** Spirituality may be more open to exploration and questioning of beliefs. It can be flexible and adaptable, allowing us to integrate various teachings and philosophies that resonate within ourselves.

- **Religion:** Religion often involves a specific set of dogmas, doctrines, and teachings that followers are expected to accept and adhere to. Questioning or deviating from these teachings may be discouraged in some religious traditions.

Focus on Inner Experience:

- **Spirituality:** Spirituality places a strong emphasis on personal inner experiences, such as self-awareness, self-discovery, and connection to higher states of consciousness. It often seeks to cultivate qualities like love, compassion, and inner peace.

- **Religion:** While inner experiences are also important in religion, the emphasis may be more on following prescribed rituals, adhering to moral codes, and seeking salvation or enlightenment through adherence to specific beliefs and practices.

Relation to Morality and Ethics:

- **Spirituality:** Spirituality often emphasizes inner growth, self-improvement, and the development of moral and ethical values. It encourages us to live in alignment with our values and principles.

- **Religion:** Religion often provides a moral and ethical framework based on its specific teachings and scriptures. Adherents are expected to follow these principles as part of their religious practice.

Community and Social Engagement:

- **Spirituality:** While spirituality can be a solitary practice, it can also lead to a sense of interconnectedness with others who share similar beliefs and values.

- **Religion:** Religion often involves active participation in a religious community, which provides a social structure and support system for its members.

It's important to note that we may identify as spiritual, religious, both, or neither. Some of us find our spiritual path within a religious tradition, while others may embrace spirituality outside of organized religion. The distinctions between spirituality and religion can be fluid and nuanced, and we may interpret and practice these concepts in various ways based on our personal beliefs and experiences.

"At any moment, you have a choice that leads you either closer or further away from your spirit."
— Thich Nhat Hanh

RECOVERY AND THE SPIRITUAL JOURNEY

How do spirituality and recovery work together?

The nature of spirituality can vary greatly from person to person, as it is influenced by individual beliefs, motivations, religious or philosophical backgrounds, and cultural contexts. Some of us may embark on a spiritual path within the framework of a particular religion or belief system, while others may explore spirituality in a more eclectic or non-traditional manner, allowing each of us the opportunity to personalize our journey based on our own understanding, experiences, and philosophical outlook.

No matter how one approaches spirituality, it involves the exploration and development of one's spiritual beliefs, practices, and understanding. This journey can be incredibly beneficial for those of us in recovery, offering support, guidance, and transformation. It provides a framework for personal growth, self-discovery, and finding meaning in our lives. Spirituality offers tools, skills, and a supportive community that can help us navigate the challenges of recovery and cultivate holistic well-being. By integrating spirituality into our healing process, we can tap into inner resources, develop resilience, and foster a deep sense of connection, purpose, and fulfillment.

Spirituality asks us to engage in self-reflection and self-discovery while exploring our values, beliefs, and behaviors to find a deeper understanding of ourselves. It provides a space to address underlying emotional wounds, trauma, unresolved issues, and fears that may have contributed to our addictive behaviors. This introspective process enables us to gain insight into the root causes of our addiction and behaviors, as well as identify patterns and triggers. Spirituality offers tools for coping with difficult issues, which can help us manage stress, regulate emotions, and find inner peace, reducing the risk of harmful behaviors or relapse.

Engaging in a spiritual path helps us find meaning and purpose. It provides a sense of direction and motivation for pursuing a healthier, more vibrant life. It often involves a search for inner peace, personal transformation, and the pursuit of enlightenment or a closer relationship with a higher power, depending on a person's religious or philosophical beliefs. This newfound focus can be a powerful motivator for us to stay committed to recovery and make positive changes as we build a strong foundation using its concepts, principles, and practices for sustained abstinence. The spiritual journey provides us with hope and inspiration toward a better way of living.

"We are not human beings having a spiritual experience; we are spiritual beings having a human experience." — Pierre Teilhard de Chardin

SPIRITUAL CONCEPTS, PRINCIPLES, AND PRACTICES

What are spiritual concepts, principles, and practices?

Spiritual concepts, principles, and practices are distinct aspects of spirituality that together contribute to a holistic and meaningful exploration of one's spiritual path.

- **Spiritual Concepts:** Spiritual concepts are abstract ideas and beliefs that form the foundation of spiritual understanding. These are universal meanings that transcend specific religious or cultural contexts and are often focused on higher truths, the nature of existence, and the interconnectedness of all things. Examples of spiritual concepts include the belief in a higher power, the concept of enlightenment, the idea of self-realization, and the recognition of the mind-body-soul connection. These concepts provide a framework for us to contemplate life's deeper questions and explore our relationship with the universe and the divine.

- **Spiritual Principles**: Spiritual principles are ethical and moral guidelines that help us live in alignment with our spiritual beliefs and values. These principles often derive from spiritual teachings and aim to promote virtues such as compassion, forgiveness, gratitude, and love. They provide a moral compass for us on our spiritual journey, guiding our actions and interactions with others. Spiritual principles encourage us to live with integrity, honesty, kindness, and an open heart, fostering a sense of harmony and interconnectedness with all living beings.

- **Spiritual Practices:** Spiritual practices are the practical rituals, activities, and disciplines that we engage in to cultivate our spiritual growth and connection. These practices can vary widely and are often rooted in specific religious traditions or spiritual teachings. Examples of spiritual practices include meditation, prayer, mindfulness movement, self-care, sacred rituals, and acts of service. Engaging in these practices allows us to deepen our spiritual awareness, develop inner peace, and nurture a sense of inner strength and resilience.

In essence, spiritual concepts provide the philosophical foundation, spiritual principles offer ethical guidelines, and spiritual practices provide the practical means for us to explore, embody, and cultivate our spirituality in a meaningful and transformative way. Together, these elements form a comprehensive and integrated approach to spirituality, supporting us on our journey of self-discovery, inner growth, and connection to a higher power.

"The purpose of spiritual awakening is not to escape the world, but to bring light and consciousness to every corner of it, leading to enlightenment." — Eckhart Tolle

SPIRITUAL CONCEPTS

SPIRITUAL AWAKENING VS. ENLIGHTENMENT

What are the spiritual concepts of spiritual awakening and enlightenment?

- **Spiritual awakening:** A spiritual awakening is a profound shift in consciousness that can occur suddenly or gradually, resulting in a transformative change in how we perceive reality. It can be triggered by various factors, such as a life-altering event, a moment of crisis, a deep spiritual experience, or dedicated spiritual practices like meditation or prayer. During a spiritual awakening, we may experience heightened awareness and a profound connection to the spiritual dimensions of existence.

The experience of a spiritual awakening can vary significantly from person to person. Some may have a sudden moment of insight, while others may undergo a gradual process of self-discovery and spiritual growth. Common characteristics of a spiritual awakening include increased mindfulness, enhanced compassion for oneself and others, a deeper sense of purpose, and a feeling of being interconnected with something greater than oneself.

Spiritual awakening is often considered a stepping stone on the path to spiritual growth and self-realization. It opens the door to deeper exploration of spiritual practices, self-reflection, and the pursuit of higher truths. Those who undergo a spiritual awakening embark on a journey of self-discovery, seeking to understand their true nature and the deeper meaning of life.

- **Enlightenment:** Enlightenment, on the other hand, is regarded as the ultimate realization in many spiritual traditions. It is described as a state of complete and permanent awakening in which one transcends the limitations of the ego and experiences profound unity with all of existence. In certain Eastern spiritual traditions, enlightenment represents the ultimate goal of human life, signifying liberation from the cycle of suffering and rebirth (Samsara).

Enlightenment is characterized by profound wisdom and understanding, i.e., perceiving the interconnectedness and interdependence of all things. It is accompanied by a deep sense of inner peace, contentment, and unconditional love for all beings. In this state, we experience profound freedom from attachment, desire, and suffering.

Unlike a spiritual awakening, which may be a temporary or intermittent experience, enlightenment is considered a permanent and irreversible state of consciousness. It brings about a fundamental transformation in the way we perceive and interact with the world.

In summary, spiritual awakening is a transformative experience that sets us on a path of self-realization and spiritual growth. It serves as a stepping stone towards deeper insights and understanding. Enlightenment, on the other hand, represents the ultimate goal of spiritual realization in many traditions—an enduring state of complete awakening that brings profound wisdom, inner peace, and liberation from suffering.

"The most important relationship we can all have is the one you have with yourself. The most important journey you can take is one of self-discovery."
— Aristotle

SELF-REALIZATION

What is the spiritual concept of self-realization?

Self-realization refers to the ongoing process of gaining a deep and profound understanding of ourselves, our true nature, and our purpose in life. It is a journey of self-discovery that goes beyond the surface-level aspects of identity and delves into the core essence of who we truly are. Self-realization involves recognizing and accepting our strengths and weaknesses and our fears and desires, as well as embracing the totality of our being. It is a continuous process of becoming more self-aware, gaining greater emotional intelligence, and striving for personal excellence.

During the process of self-realization, we may become aware of our limiting beliefs, conditioning, and patterns of behavior that have shaped our identity. We may explore past traumas and unresolved emotions, allowing for healing and personal growth. Self-realization also involves understanding the roles and masks we may have adopted to fit societal expectations or cope with challenges.

Through self-realization, we can develop a sense of inner clarity, authenticity, and purpose. It is a transformative journey that leads to greater self-awareness, self-acceptance, and self-compassion. As we gain insights into our true nature, we can live a life that is congruent with our deepest truths, values, and aspirations, fostering a sense of inner harmony and contentment.

How does self-realization help recovery?

- **Awareness of the underlying causes**: Self-realization involves deep self-examination. It allows us to explore the root causes and triggers of our addictions. Understanding these underlying factors is essential for effective recovery, as they provide insight into why addictive behaviors developed in the first place.

- **Personal responsibility:** Self-realization fosters a sense of personal responsibility. It empowers us to take ownership of our actions and decisions, including those that led to addiction. This acknowledgment is a pivotal step towards recovery, as it shifts the focus from external blame to internal accountability.

- **Motivation for change:** Realizing the impact of addiction on our lives and the lives of loved ones can be a powerful motivator for change. Self-realization often brings clarity about the need for recovery and the desire to make positive changes.

- **Increased self-esteem:** Self-realization can boost self-esteem and self-worth. As we begin to understand ourselves on a deeper level and accept our imperfections, we often experience a renewed sense of value and self-respect.

- **Emotional healing:** Addiction is often accompanied by emotional wounds and unresolved traumas. Self-realization provides a platform for emotional healing. It allows us to process past experiences, release pent-up emotions, and develop healthier coping strategies.

- **Improved relationships:** A deeper understanding of our selves can lead to healthier relationships with others. Self-realization often promotes better communication, empathy, and the ability to establish boundaries, contributing to more supportive and fulfilling connections.

- **Spiritual growth:** For many, self-realization is intertwined with spiritual growth. It can lead to a deeper connection with our spiritual beliefs or a search for higher meaning. This spiritual aspect can provide a source of strength and guidance in recovery.

- **Long-term recovery:** Self-realization is not just a short-term benefit; it forms the foundation for long-term recovery. It equips us with self-awareness, coping skills, and a commitment to personal growth, all of which are essential for sustained sobriety.

What are ways to cultivate self-realization?

- **Self-reflection***:* Regularly set aside time for introspection and self-reflection. Journaling can be a valuable tool to record your thoughts, feelings, and insights about yourself and your life experiences.

- **Mindfulness meditation***:* Mindfulness practices, including meditation, can help you become more aware of your thoughts, emotions, and bodily sensations. This heightened awareness can lead to greater self-understanding.

- **Therapy and counseling***:* Professional therapy or counseling sessions provide a safe and supportive space to explore your thoughts, emotions, and behaviors. A therapist can guide you in the process of self-discovery.

- **Reading and learning***:* Engage in self-help books, articles, and resources that focus on personal growth, self-awareness, and self-realization. Learning from the experiences of others can provide valuable insights into your own journey.

- **Seek feedback:** Ask for feedback from trusted friends, family members, or mentors. They may offer perspectives on your strengths, weaknesses, and areas for growth that you haven't considered.

- ⚘ **Mind-body practices**: Practices like yoga, Tai Chi, or qigong can help you connect with your body and emotions, facilitating self-awareness and self-realization.

- ⚘ **Creative expression**: Engage in creative activities like writing, painting, music, or dancing. Creative outlets can help you express your thoughts and emotions in unique and insightful ways.

- ⚘ **Connect with nature**: Spending time in nature can be grounding and provide moments of clarity and self-realization. Nature has a way of inspiring introspection.

- ⚘ **Mindful relationships**: Pay attention to your interactions with others. Healthy relationships can offer mirrors for self-reflection and personal growth.

- ⚘ **Stay curious:** Cultivate a curious mindset. Be open to exploring new experiences, perspectives, and knowledge. Curiosity can lead to self-discovery.

Self-realization is a transformative process that supports recovery by fostering awareness, responsibility, motivation, and emotional healing. It empowers us to break free from destructive patterns, rebuild self-esteem, and develop healthier relationships. Ultimately, self-realization is a powerful tool for achieving and maintaining lasting sobriety and well-being. Remember that self-realization is a unique journey for each person. There is no fixed timeline, and it's okay to seek support and guidance along the way. Be gentle with yourself, stay committed to the process, and embrace the wisdom and self-awareness that come with self-realization.

"A fight is going on inside me,' said an old man to his son. 'It is a terrible fight between two wolves. One wolf is evil. He is anger, envy, sorrow, regret, greed, arrogance, self-pity, guilt, resentment, inferiority, lies, false pride, superiority, and ego. The other wolf is good. He is joy, peace, love, hope, serenity, humility, kindness, benevolence, empathy, generosity, truth, compassion, and faith. The same fight is going on inside you.' The son thought about it for a minute and then asked, 'Which wolf will win?' The old man replied simply, 'The one you feed.'"
- Wendy Mass

EGO AND FALSE PRIDE

What are the spiritual concepts of ego and false pride?

Ego and false pride are interconnected and relate to the way we perceive and identify ourselves. Here's an explanation of each:

- **Ego:** In spiritual contexts, the ego refers to the sense of self, or the "I," that we commonly identify with. It is the mental construct of our individual identity, consisting of our thoughts, beliefs, emotions, and self-image. The ego is the part of our consciousness that often seeks validation, recognition, and gratification, leading to desires, attachments, and fears.

  In spiritual teachings, the ego is seen as the source of suffering and the illusion of separateness. It creates a false sense of self-importance and can lead to selfishness, judgment, and the perception of superiority or inferiority. The ego's constant need for validation and control can result in inner conflict and dissatisfaction, hindering our spiritual growth and connection with others and the universe.

- **False pride:** False pride is a particular aspect of the ego in which we develop an inflated sense of self-worth based on external achievements, possessions, or perceived superiority over others. It involves being overly attached to our accomplishments or external validation to boost self-esteem.

False pride often leads to arrogance, boasting, and the need to prove ourselves to others, which can create a disconnect from genuine self-worth and authentic relationships. In spiritual terms, false pride is considered an obstacle to self-awareness and spiritual growth because it reinforces the ego's illusion of separateness and reinforces the idea that our worth is contingent on external factors.

Both the concepts of ego and false pride are explored in various spiritual and philosophical traditions as obstacles that we must overcome to attain higher levels of consciousness, inner peace, and genuine connection with others and the divine. Letting go of false pride and transcending the limitations of the ego are seen as essential steps toward spiritual awakening and true self-realization. By embracing humility, authenticity, and compassion, we can free ourselves from the trappings of ego-driven desires and cultivate a deeper sense of inner harmony and spiritual connection.

Why is it important to learn about both ego and false pride in recovery?

- **Self-awareness:** Recovery often involves a journey of self-discovery and self-awareness. Learning about the ego and false pride can help us recognize our own patterns of thinking and behavior that might have contributed to our addiction or other negative behaviors. This self-awareness is essential for making lasting changes.

- **Identifying triggers:** Ego and false pride can be triggers for relapse. For example, if your ego is tied to the idea that you have control over your substance use, you might resist seeking help or following a recovery plan. False pride can prevent you from admitting you have a problem or seeking support from others. Understanding these triggers can help you recognize when your ego or false pride is taking over and potentially sabotaging your recovery efforts.

- **Humility:** Recovery often involves letting go of the need to be in control and embracing humility. Ego and false pride can hinder this process by making you resistant to acknowledging your mistakes or seeking guidance. Understanding these concepts can encourage you to let go of your ego-driven behaviors and approach your recovery with a more open mind and willingness to learn from others.

- **Relationships:** Ego and false pride can strain relationships, both during active addiction and in recovery. People struggling with ego might struggle to admit wrongdoing or apologize, while false pride can prevent us from mending broken relationships. Learning about these concepts can help those of us in recovery recognize the importance of humility and vulnerability in repairing and maintaining healthy relationships.

- **Personal growth:** Recovery is not just about quitting a substance; it's also about personal growth and transformation. Understanding the ego and false pride can be a stepping stone toward personal development, as you learn to let go of limiting beliefs and behaviors that have held you back.

- **Preventing relapse:** Relapse can occur when you fall back into old patterns of thinking and behavior. Recognizing the role that ego and false pride play in these patterns can empower you to actively work on countering them and reducing the risk of relapse.

- **Coping strategies:** Learning about the ego and false pride can provide us with valuable coping strategies. When we encounter situations where our ego is challenged or false pride is at play, we can use the knowledge we've gained to navigate those situations in healthier ways.

What are ways to let go of ego and false pride?

- **Self-reflection:** Take time to examine your thoughts, actions, and reactions. Be honest with yourself about any ego-driven behaviors or beliefs that may be hindering your growth.

- **Practicing humility:** Embrace the concept of humility and recognize that you are not perfect. Accept your flaws and limitations with compassion and understanding.

- **Cultivating empathy:** Put yourself in others' shoes and try to understand their perspectives and experiences. Empathy fosters connection and helps dissolve barriers created by the ego.

- **Practicing mindfulness:** Be present in the moment and observe your thoughts and emotions without judgment. Mindfulness allows you to become more aware of ego-driven patterns.

- **Surrendering control:** Recognize that there are aspects of life beyond your control. Embrace uncertainty and trust in the natural flow of life.

- **Embracing vulnerability:** Allow yourself to be vulnerable and open with others. Embracing vulnerability creates deeper connections and dissolves the need for self-protection.

- **Letting go of comparison:** Avoid comparing yourself to others. Recognize that each individual's journey is unique and focus on your own growth and progress.

- **Seeking feedback:** Be open to receiving constructive feedback from others. Constructive criticism can help you identify ego-driven behaviors and provide opportunities for growth.

- 🌿 **Practicing gratitude:** Cultivate a sense of gratitude for the people and experiences in your life. Gratitude shifts the focus from ego-driven desires to appreciation for what you already have.

- 🌿 **Engaging in service:** Get involved in acts of service and helping others. Serving others promotes humility and allows you to connect with a larger purpose beyond the self.

Overall, understanding the ego and false pride can contribute to a more well-rounded and effective recovery process. It encourages self-reflection, humility, and personal growth, all of which are essential components of long-term recovery and positive life change. Remember that letting go of ego and false pride is a continuous process. Be patient with yourself and celebrate every small step you take towards greater self-awareness and growth. Embrace the journey with kindness and compassion for yourself and others.

"Your higher self is always guiding you towards growth, expansion, and love. Listen to its whispers within your heart." – Unknown

HIGHER SELF

What is the spiritual concept of a higher self?

The higher self is a profound concept in spiritual and philosophical teachings, representing a part of us that transcends everyday consciousness and ego. This attribute in oneself is seen as a deeper, more authentic aspect that connects us to universal truths and the interconnectedness of all life. Unlike the ego, which is tied to one's identity and physical presence, the higher self embodies a broader, more holistic perspective. It is often described as a source of inner wisdom, intuition, and spiritual insight, acting like an inner compass that guides us toward growth, understanding, and enlightenment. This side of us is also associated with elevated qualities such as unconditional love, compassion, and a deep, empathetic understanding of life.

Engagement with the higher self is linked to personal growth and spiritual development. It typically involves introspection, meditation, and other spiritual practices that foster a deeper connection with this inner dimension. Those of us who successfully connect with our higher selves often experience a heightened sense of inner peace, purpose, and alignment with our true values and life path. In essence, the higher self represents a more authentic and spiritually connected aspect of being, offering guidance and wisdom far beyond the ordinary scope of everyday self-awareness.

How does connecting with our higher selves help recovery?

- **Purpose and direction:** Connecting with the higher self provides a profound sense of purpose and alignment with one's values and life path, fostering commitment to recovery goals.

- **Self-compassion and love:** Embracing qualities associated with the higher self, like love and compassion, helps cultivate self-compassion and transform negative self-perceptions from addiction.

- **Transcending ego:** Recognizing the higher self as being beyond ego limitations allows detachment from destructive thoughts and behaviors, encouraging forgiveness and a focus on the present.

- **Strength in challenges:** The higher self offers strength and guidance during difficult times, enhancing resilience and inner peace in the face of obstacles.

- **Spiritual nature:** Embracing the higher self reinforces the idea of a deeper spiritual nature and potential for growth beyond addiction, instilling hope and inspiration.

- **Deeper connection:** By tapping into the higher self, we can find a profound connection to something greater, aiding our journey towards lasting sobriety and holistic well-being.

- **Positive perspective shift:** Engaging with the higher self can help shift perspectives from negativity and limitation to positivity and possibility, which is vital for overcoming the mindset often associated with addiction.

- **Guidance and insight:** The higher self is often seen as a source of wisdom. Connecting with it can provide clarity, guidance, and insights, which can be crucial in navigating the complex journey of recovery.

What are ways to connect with the higher self?

- **Meditation:** Regular meditation helps quiet the mind, allowing you to tune in to your higher self. This can be through guided meditations, mindfulness practices, or silent contemplation.

- **Mindfulness:** Practicing mindfulness throughout the day keeps you present and aware, making it easier to recognize the voice of your higher self amidst daily distractions.

- **Introspection:** Engage in self-reflection to explore your beliefs, desires, and life purpose, allowing your higher self to reveal insights.

- **Journaling:** Write down your thoughts, feelings, and inspirations to gain clarity and receive messages from your higher self.

- **Nature immersion:** Spending time in nature can be grounding and enlightening, helping you feel more connected to your higher self. The tranquility of natural settings often facilitates deeper introspection.

- **Creative expression:** Engaging in creative activities like painting, writing, or music can open up channels to your higher self, as these activities often bypass the rational mind and tap into deeper insights.

- **Prayer or affirmations:** Speak from your heart, expressing gratitude, intentions, or affirmations to strengthen your connection with your higher self.

- **Trusting intuition:** Practice listening to your inner voice and trusting the intuitive guidance from your higher self.

- **Silence and solitude:** Create moments of stillness and solitude to tune in to the subtle messages from your higher self.

- **Cultivate love and compassion:** Embrace self-love and compassion for others, as these qualities resonate with the essence of your higher self.

Each of these practices helps to quiet the mind, open the heart, and align your daily consciousness with the wisdom and insight of your higher self. Connecting with one's higher self in recovery can offer profound insights, emotional support, and a stronger sense of inner peace and resilience, all of which are crucial components in the journey towards healing and personal growth. The key is to find what resonates with you and make it a regular part of your practice.

"Believe in a higher power; believe in something outside yourself, something bigger than your circumstances." — Nick Vujicic

HIGHER POWER

What is the spiritual concept of a higher power?

A higher power represents a profound a force or presence that transcends the material world and holds significant influence over the universe and human existence. It is a central tenet in many spiritual and religious traditions, with interpretations varying widely. At its core, the concept of a higher power acknowledges the limitations of human understanding and control, recognizing that there are aspects of existence that extend beyond the grasp of the physical and rational realms.

A higher power is frequently associated with notions of divinity, encompassing beliefs in a singular god, multiple deities, cosmic consciousness, or even a universal life force. It embodies qualities of transcendence and omnipotence, suggesting that this force exists beyond the confines of space and time and possesses the ability to shape the cosmos and the course of human lives. Belief in a higher power often extends to the idea that it can offer guidance, support, and a sense of purpose, encouraging us to align our actions with spiritual values and principles. Ultimately, the spiritual concept of a higher power provides a framework for understanding the mysteries of existence, finding meaning in life, and seeking a connection with a greater, transcendent reality.

What are examples of a higher power?

- **God or deities from various religious traditions:** These are the supreme beings or divine entities worshipped in different religions such as Christianity (God), Islam (Allah), Judaism (Yahweh), Hinduism (Brahman, Vishnu, Shiva, etc.),

Buddhism (various Buddhas), and so on. They are often considered omnipotent, omniscient, and omnipresent, shaping the beliefs, practices, and moral codes of their respective religions.

- **The Divine or the Universe:** This refers to a concept of a sacred and transcendent force or entity that is often seen as the ultimate source of creation, existence, and order in the cosmos. It encompasses spiritual, mystical, or religious notions of a higher power that governs all life and phenomena.

- **Nature:** Nature refers to the natural world, including elements such as plants, animals, landscapes, and eco-systems. Connecting with nature involves appreciating its beauty, harmony, and interconnectedness, often seen as a reflection of a higher power or divine presence.

- **Collective consciousness:** This is the idea that there is a shared or collective awareness, beliefs, and knowledge among a group of individuals or within a society. It empha-sizes the interconnectedness of human experience and the power of community in shaping thoughts, values, and actions.

- **Inner strength:** Inner strength refers to the resilience, courage, and determination found within oneself. It can be seen as a manifestation of a higher power or inner spiritual force that enables individuals to overcome challenges, pursue growth, and maintain integrity.

- **Love and compassion:** Love and compassion are regarded as powerful forces that guide moral behavior, empathy, and kindness towards others. They are often considered essential aspects of spiritual growth and connection to a higher power.

- **Higher self:** The higher self is a concept in spirituality and psychology that refers to a transcendent or elevated aspect of one's identity beyond the ego. It is associated with inner wisdom, intuition, and a deeper understanding of spiritual truths and purpose.

- **Spirit guides or angels:** These are spiritual beings believed to provide guidance, protection, and support to individuals on their spiritual journey. They are often seen as intermediaries between humans and the divine realm.

- **Ancestral spirits:** Ancestral spirits are the spirits of deceased ancestors, revered and honored in many cultures for their wisdom, guidance, and connection to familial heritage and traditions.

- **Universal laws:** Universal laws are fundamental principles or rules believed to govern the functioning of the universe, such as karma (the law of cause and effect), the law of attraction, and other metaphysical or cosmic principles.

- **Life force energy:** Also known as chi, prana, or vital energy, life force energy is a concept in various spiritual and healing traditions that refers to the vital energy that animates living beings and sustains life.

- **Music or art:** Music and art are forms of creative expression that can evoke spiritual or transcendent experiences, offering a means of connecting with a higher power or expressing one's spiritual insights and emotions.

- **Truth and wisdom:** Truth and wisdom are universal concepts that represent the pursuit of knowledge, understanding, and enlightenment. They often serve as guiding principles in spiritual and philosophical exploration.

- **Higher consciousness:** Higher consciousness refers to an expanded state of awareness, insight, and perception beyond ordinary consciousness. It involves spiritual awakening, self-realization, and a deeper connection to the divine or transcendent aspects of existence.

- **The greater good:** The greater good emphasizes the idea of prioritizing collective well-being, harmony, and social justice over individual interests. It reflects a spiritual or ethical principle of considering the interconnectedness and interdependence of all beings.

- **Synchronicities:** Synchronicities are meaningful coincidences or events that seem to be interconnected or guided by a higher intelligence or spiritual force, often interpreted as signs or messages on one's spiritual path.

- **Personal values and principles:** These are the beliefs, morals, and ethical standards that guide an individual's behavior, choices, and interactions with others. They often reflect one's spiritual or philosophical outlook.

- **Scientific method:** The scientific method is a systematic approach to inquiry and problem-solving in science. It involves making observations, formulating hypotheses, conducting experiments, collecting data, and using evidence-based reasoning to draw conclusions.

- **Natural laws:** Natural laws are the fundamental principles that govern the physical universe, including laws of physics (e.g., gravity, thermodynamics), chemistry (e.g., chemical reactions), and biology (e.g., evolution, genetics). They describe the regularities and patterns observed in nature's behavior.

How does belief in a higher power help recovery?

- **Promotes recognition of personal limitations:** As we embrace the belief in a higher power, we begin to recognize our own limitations. This realization is integral to the recovery process, as it prompts us to acknowledge that we cannot overcome our challenges entirely on our own. We begin to understand the need for external support and guidance.

- **Fosters humility and openness:** Belief in a higher power fosters a sense of humility by acknowledging that there is something greater than ourselves. This humility, in turn, opens us to receiving help and guidance from others, whether it's from a support group, therapist, or treatment program. It allows us to admit that we don't have all the answers and can benefit from the wisdom of others.

- **Provides solace and comfort:** Belief in a higher power offers solace and comfort during difficult times. It provides a framework for making sense of life's challenges and finding meaning in adversity. This spiritual connection can be a source of emotional strength, helping us maintain resilience and preventing relapse during challenging moments.

- **Moral and ethical framework:** The higher power often serves as a basis for moral and ethical principles. We may look to our higher power for guidance on what is right and wrong and strive to align our actions with these principles.

- **Forgiveness and redemption:** Many belief systems with a higher power incorporate concepts of forgiveness and redemption. We may seek forgiveness from our higher power for past wrongs and view our relationship with this power as a path to personal transformation and growth.

- **Purpose and meaning:** Belief in a higher power often provides us with a sense of purpose and meaning in life. It gives our existence deeper significance and encourages us to live in a way that reflects our spiritual values.

- **Surrender and trust:** A common theme in recovery and spirituality is the idea of surrendering control and placing trust in a higher power. This act of surrender is seen as a way to release burdens and find acceptance and peace.

- **Freedom and liberation:** Some spiritual concepts of a higher power emphasize the idea of liberation, or freedom from suffering and attachment. It's viewed as a path to transcend the limitations and challenges of human existence.

- **Source of guidance:** Many of us view our higher power as a source of guidance and wisdom. We turn to this higher power for direction in our lives, seeking answers to important questions and decisions.

What are ways to connect with a higher power?

- **Self-reflection:** Take time to reflect on your beliefs, values, and experiences. Consider what resonates with you and what you find meaningful. Reflect on moments when you've felt a sense of connection or transcendence.

- **Open-mindedness:** Approach the search for a higher power with an open mind. Be willing to explore different perspectives and ideas, even if they differ from your current beliefs.

- **Exploration:** Research different spiritual and philosophical traditions to gain insight into how they define and connect with a higher power. This exploration can provide you with a broader perspective.

- **Nature and Universe:** Many people find a sense of the divine or higher power in the beauty and complexity of the natural world. Spending time in nature and observing its wonders can be a way to connect.

- **Personal experiences:** Reflect on moments in your life when you've felt a sense of guidance, synchronicity, or something greater than yourself at play. These experiences can offer clues about your higher power.

- **Intuition:** Trust your intuition. Pay attention to what resonates with you on a deep level, even if it doesn't necessarily fit into a predefined religious or spiritual framework.

- **Meditation and prayer:** Engage in meditation or prayer to create a space for connection and reflection. This can provide insights and help you feel more attuned to a higher power.

- **Community:** Engage with spiritual or religious communities that align with your beliefs. Sharing experiences and having discussions with like-minded individuals can provide guidance and support.

- **Inner guidance:** Pay attention to your inner voice and intuition. Sometimes, the answers you seek come from within when you allow yourself to listen.

- **Art and creativity:** Engaging in creative activities such as art, writing, or music can help you tap into your inner self and explore your relationship with a higher power.

- **Service to others:** Helping others and engaging in acts of kindness can create a sense of connection to something greater than yourself and can lead you to a deeper understanding of your higher power.

- **Acceptance of mystery:** Recognize that the nature of a higher power may be mysterious and beyond complete comprehension. Allow room for the unknown and the mystical.

It's important to note that the concept of a higher power(s) is highly individualized and can be shaped by one's religious or spiritual beliefs, personal experiences, and cultural background. What is meaningful and relevant as a higher power can vary greatly from person to person and can evolve over time. For some of us, there may be a connection with more than one form of higher power. The most important thing is to approach your search with an open heart and a willingness to connect with something that resonates with your inner self and values.

> *"Sometimes we need divine will to protect us from our free will. Divine intervention is never a heavenly punishment or transcendental prank. It is a safeguard for our highest good."*
> — Anthon St. Maarten

DIVINE INTERVENTION

What is the spiritual concept of divine intervention?

Divine intervention refers to the belief or concept that a higher power, deity, God, or divine force intervenes in human affairs to bring about a specific outcome or to provide guidance, protection, or assistance in times of need. It suggests that there are moments when a higher power directly influences events or circumstances in the world, often in ways that are beyond human understanding or explanation.

The idea of divine intervention is prevalent in various religious and spiritual traditions. It is often seen as a sign of divine presence, benevolence, and care for individuals or humanity as a whole. People may interpret divine intervention as a miraculous occurrence, a timely coincidence, or a series of events that lead to a desired outcome, attributing it to the workings of a higher power.

Those of us who believe in divine intervention may seek solace, hope, and guidance during challenging times, relying on the idea that a higher power is watching over us and intervening in our lives. It can provide a sense of comfort and reassurance, especially when facing difficult circumstances or making significant life decisions.

However, the concept of divine intervention can be subjective and open to interpretation, as beliefs about the nature and extent of divine involvement can vary among different religious and spiritual traditions. Some see divine intervention as an active and ongoing presence in daily life, while others view it as a more subtle or mysterious force that operates in ways beyond human comprehension.

How does belief in divine intervention help recovery?

- **Source of support and hope:** The belief in a higher power actively involved in our recovery journey through divine intervention offers a source of comfort, guidance, and hope beyond personal capabilities. This can serve as a guiding light during challenging times, instilling confidence that help is available even when things seem difficult.

- **Release of control:** Recognizing the presence of divine intervention encourages us to let go of the need for complete control over our recovery. This surrender to a higher power allows us to rely on external assistance, reducing feelings of pressure and self-reliance.

- **Stress reduction:** Believing in divine intervention can help alleviate stress and anxiety by fostering the assurance that there is a benevolent force working in our favor. This sense of trust and protection can contribute to overall emotional well-being.

- **Guidance in decision-making:** Many of us in recovery face pivotal decisions that impact our sobriety. Belief in divine intervention can provide guidance and clarity, helping us make choices that align with our recovery goals and spiritual values.

- **Overcoming challenges:** The notion of divine intervention inspires resilience and determination. We may draw strength from the belief that we are not alone in our struggles and that a higher power is supporting us through adversity.

- **Cultivation of faith:** Believing in divine intervention nurtures faith in a higher purpose. This faith can motivate us to persist in our recovery journey, even when faced with setbacks or uncertainty.

- **Sense of meaning:** Belief in divine intervention infuses the recovery journey with a sense of purpose and significance. It reinforces the idea that our struggles are part of a larger plan aimed at growth, healing, and self-discovery.

- **Building resilience:** The knowledge that a higher power is watching over can provide us with the strength to navigate challenges, resist triggers, and maintain our commitment to sobriety.

- **Connection to something greater:** Embracing divine intervention fosters a sense of connection to a greater spiritual realm, helping us feel part of something larger than ourselves. This connection can provide solace and a sense of belonging.

What are ways to experience divine intervention?

- **Synchronicities:** Meaningful coincidences or synchronicities that align with our recovery path, such as encountering a relevant book, meeting someone who shares our struggles, or experiencing a timely event that offers guidance.

- **Intuition and inner guidance:** A heightened sense of intuition or inner knowing that guides us toward healthy choices, helping us make decisions aligned with our recovery goals.

- **Unexpected encounters:** Chance encounters with people who provide encouragement, inspiration, or information that proves invaluable to our recovery journey.

- **Inner peace and calm:** Moments of unexpected peace and calm during challenging times, offering a sense of reassurance and support when needed most.

- ❧ **Answered prayers:** Experiencing situations where prayers or intentions are seemingly answered, providing a tangible sense of connection to a higher power.

- ❧ **Symbolic messages:** Encountering symbols, signs, or messages in their environment that hold personal significance and provide guidance or encouragement.

- ❧ **Inspirational insights:** Receiving sudden insights or revelations that shed light on aspects of our recovery, offering clarity and direction.

- ❧ **Divine timing:** Experiencing events unfolding in a way that seems perfectly timed and aligned with our recovery needs.

- ❧ **Emotional shifts:** Undergoing transformative emotional shifts or breakthroughs that lead to healing, growth, and positive change.

- ❧ **Aligned opportunities:** Encountering opportunities or circumstances that align with our recovery goals, offering a sense of purpose and direction.

While these experiences may vary for each of us, they collectively contribute to a sense of connection with a higher power and a deepened belief in the role of divine intervention in our recovery journey. Overall, belief in divine intervention offers emotional, psychological, and spiritual support that complements other aspects of the recovery process, enhancing our ability to overcome challenges and maintain a fulfilling life of sobriety.

"We are not separate from each other or from the world. We are a part of it all, and it is a part of us."
— *Thich Nhat Hanh*

UNITY

What is the spiritual concept of unity?

Unity revolves around the understanding that all things in existence are interconnected and part of a larger, divine whole. It emphasizes the idea that we are not separate entities but rather interconnected beings, all sharing the same source of consciousness or divine energy.

In spiritual teachings, unity signifies the oneness of all life and the recognition that there is a deeper underlying reality that connects everything and everyone. It transcends individual differences, divisions, and separateness, promoting a sense of harmony, love, and compassion for all living beings. The concept of unity encourages us to see beyond superficial distinctions and to embrace the underlying unity that binds all of creation together. It fosters a profound sense of interconnectedness, empathy, and understanding, encouraging us to treat others with kindness and respect.

For many spiritual traditions, the journey towards unity involves inner exploration and self-discovery, leading to a deeper connection with the divine or universal consciousness. It is believed that through this realization of unity, we can experience a profound transformation, finding purpose, peace, and a sense of belonging in the greater cosmic tapestry of existence.

Ultimately, the spiritual meaning of unity invites us to recognize our interconnectedness with all life, transcending ego-driven separateness and promoting a higher level of consciousness that embraces love, compassion, and the collective well-being of all beings.

How does unity help recovery?

- **Overcoming isolation:** In recovery, we might feel isolated due to the stigma surrounding addiction or the sense of alienation from others. Embracing the concept of unity helps us realize that we are not alone in our struggles. It fosters a sense of belonging and interconnectedness with others who have experienced similar challenges, creating a supportive community.

- **Reducing judgment:** Unity teaches acceptance and compassion for all beings. By embracing this concept, those of us in recovery can let go of self-judgment and reduce our judgment of others. This self-compassion is essential for healing from past mistakes and developing a healthier self-image.

- **Building supportive relationships:** The idea of unity encourages us to see the interconnectedness between ourselves and others. This realization promotes the cultivation of healthy and supportive relationships, ones in which we can rely on each other for encouragement and growth.

- **Finding purpose and meaning:** Understanding unity can lead to a greater sense of purpose and meaning in recovery. Recognizing that everyone is connected and part of a larger whole can inspire us to strive for personal growth and contribute positively to the collective well-being.

- **Embracing higher power:** For those of us who believe in a higher power or divine energy, unity reinforces the idea that we are connected to something greater than ourselves. This connection can provide comfort, guidance, and strength during challenging times in the recovery process.

- **Promoting emotional healing:** The sense of interconnectedness in unity can foster empathy and understanding, creating a safe space for emotional expression and healing. It allows us to share our experiences, vulnerabilities, and triumphs, leading to emotional growth.

- **Transcending ego:** Unity encourages us to move beyond the limitations of the ego and embrace a higher level of consciousness. This shift can help us let go of pride, arrogance, and self-centeredness, promoting humility and openness to change.

- **Inspiring service and giving:** The recognition of unity can inspire us to give back and help others who are facing similar challenges. It encourages acts of service and compassion, which can be empowering and fulfilling.

What are ways to find and experience unity?

- **Meditation and mindfulness:** Practice meditation and mindfulness to quiet the mind, become more present, and develop a sense of inner peace and connectedness.

- **Gratitude practice:** Cultivate gratitude for the blessings in your life, acknowledging the interconnectedness of all things and the abundance that surrounds you.

- **Acts of kindness:** Engage in acts of kindness and compassion towards others, recognizing the shared humanity and interconnectedness of all beings.

- **Nature connection:** Spend time in nature and connect with the natural world to experience the beauty and unity of all living things.

- **Yoga and breathwork:** Engage in yoga and breathwork practices to harmonize the mind, body, and spirit, fostering a sense of oneness and balance.

- **Spiritual reading and reflection:** Read spiritual texts and reflect on their teachings, gaining insights into the interconnectedness of all life.

- **Attend spiritual gatherings:** Participate in spiritual gatherings or community events to connect with like-minded individuals and share in collective spiritual experiences.

- **Embrace diversity:** Celebrate diversity and appreciate the uniqueness of each individual, recognizing the unity that exists within our differences.

- **Practice self-compassion:** Be kind and compassionate towards yourself, acknowledging your inherent worth and connection to the greater whole.

- **Surrender and let go:** Practice surrendering to the flow of life and letting go of attachments, trusting in the interconnectedness of all things and the higher wisdom at play.

The spiritual concept of unity can be a powerful and transformative tool in the recovery process. It instills a sense of hope, connection, and purpose, providing us with the strength and motivation to navigate the path of recovery with a renewed sense of awareness and interconnectedness with the world around us. By incorporating these practices into your life, you can open yourself to the profound experience of spiritual unity, deepening your connection to yourself, others, and the universe, and enriching your recovery journey.

"Your mind, body, and soul are like three best friends that you should always cherish, nurture, and encourage." — Michael Lee

MIND-BODY-SOUL CONNECTION

What is the spiritual concept of mind-body-soul connection?

The mind-body-soul connection refers to the belief that the mind, body, and soul are interconnected and inseparable aspects of human existence. It suggests that these three aspects are not separate entities but rather are interconnected and influence each other, contributing to a person's overall well-being and spiritual experience.

- **The mind:** The mind represents the aspect of consciousness and cognitive processes. It includes thoughts, beliefs, emotions, perceptions, and mental activities. The mind plays a crucial role in shaping how we perceive the world, interpret experiences, and respond to various situations.

- **The body***:* The body refers to the physical vessel that houses our consciousness. It encompasses the physical senses, organs, and physiological functions. The body is a tangible and visible aspect of ourselves, and its health and well-being are influenced by various factors, including lifestyle, diet, exercise, and environmental factors.

- **The soul***:* The soul, also known as the spirit or higher self, represents the eternal and spiritual essence of us. It is often associated with our innermost being, consciousness, and connection to a higher power or divine source. The soul is considered eternal and transcends the physical realm, carrying the accumulated wisdom and experiences of multiple lifetimes, depending on our spiritual beliefs.

A balanced and harmonious connection between the mind, body, and soul is believed to promote overall well-being, personal growth, and spiritual development. Many spiritual practices and holistic approaches aim to strengthen this connection through various techniques such as meditation, mindfulness, prayer, yoga, self-reflection, and self-care. By nurturing this connection, we can achieve overall well-being.

How does a balanced mind-body-soul connection help recovery?

- **Holistic well-being:** Recovery is not solely about abstaining from substances; it involves achieving overall well-being. A balanced mind-body-soul connection addresses all aspects of health, ensuring that those of us in recovery focus not only on sobriety but also on mental, emotional, and spiritual wellness.

- **Emotional resilience:** Emotional well-being is paramount in recovery. A balanced connection helps us manage stress, anxiety, and depression more effectively, reducing the risk of relapse triggered by these emotions.

- **Physical health:** Addiction often takes a toll on physical health. Reconnecting with the body through practices like exercise, nutrition, and adequate sleep supports physical healing and enhances our sense of vitality and strength.

- **Mindfulness:** A balanced connection encourages mindfulness, which is essential for managing cravings and triggers. Mindfulness practices help us stay present, cope with stress, and make healthier choices.

- **Spiritual growth:** Spirituality offers a deeper sense of purpose and meaning. Nurturing the soul component of the connection can aid in finding that purpose, making the recovery journey more meaningful and motivating.

- **Resilience:** Strengthening the mind-body-soul connection builds resilience. We are better equipped to handle life's challenges, adapt to change, and maintain sobriety despite external stressors.

- **Healthy coping mechanisms:** A balanced connection promotes the development of healthy coping mechanisms. Instead of turning to substances, we learn to cope with difficulties through practices like meditation, exercise, and seeking support from others.

- **Reduced relapse risk:** A holistic approach to recovery addresses the root causes of addiction, reducing the risk of relapse. By balancing mental, physical, and spiritual well-being, we build a solid foundation for sustained sobriety.

- **Enhanced self-awareness:** The mind-body-soul connection encourages self-awareness. Understanding our thoughts, emotions, and spiritual needs helps us make informed choices and develop a deeper understanding of our journey.

What are ways to strengthen the mind-body-soul connection?

- **Meditation and mindfulness:** Engage in regular meditation and mindfulness practices to quiet the mind, increase self-awareness, and foster a deeper connection with your inner self.

- **Physical exercise:** Incorporate regular physical activities that you enjoy, such as yoga, walking, or dancing, to keep your body healthy and promote a sense of vitality.

- **Balanced nutrition:** Pay attention to your diet and aim to consume nourishing, whole foods that support your physical and mental well-being.

- **Adequate rest and sleep:** Prioritize sufficient sleep and rest to rejuvenate your body and mind, allowing for better emotional regulation and mental clarity.

- **Self-reflection:** Set aside time for self-reflection, journaling, or introspection to gain insights into your emotions, thoughts, and beliefs.

- **Practice gratitude:** Cultivate a daily practice of gratitude to shift your focus towards positive aspects of life, promoting a sense of contentment and well-being.

- **Creative expression:** Engage in creative activities that resonate with your soul, such as writing, painting, or playing music, to tap into your inner wisdom and emotions.

- **Mindful breathing:** Practice deep breathing exercises to ground yourself in the present moment and reduce stress and anxiety.

- **Connect with nature:** Spend time in nature to experience a sense of interconnectedness and find peace and solace.

- **Cultivate spirituality:** Explore spiritual practices or beliefs that resonate with you, whether through religious practices, prayer, or connection with a higher power.

- **Seek support:** Build a strong support network by connecting with like-minded individuals, seeking therapy or counseling, or participating in support groups.

- **Set boundaries:** Establish healthy boundaries in relationships and situations to protect your well-being and energy.

- **Let go of negativity:** Release negative thought patterns and beliefs that no longer serve you and replace them with positive affirmations.

- **Engage in acts of kindness:** Practice acts of kindness and compassion towards yourself and others, fostering a sense of interconnectedness and empathy.

- ❧ **Limit technology:** Take breaks from technology and spend time disconnected to allow yourself to be fully present in the moment.

- ❧ **Create a holistic routine:** Incorporate activities that nourish all three aspects of your being into your daily routine.

- ❧ **Self-care:** Set aside time for activities that bring joy, relaxation, and fulfillment.

By integrating these practices into our daily lives, we can nurture and strengthen the mind-body-soul connection. A balanced mind-body-soul connection is integral to recovery as it addresses the physical, mental, emotional, and spiritual aspects of well-being. It enhances resilience, reduces relapse risk, fosters healthy coping mechanisms, and promotes holistic health and a deeper sense of purpose. Ultimately, it helps us not just survive but thrive on our sobriety journey.

*"Honesty is the best policy. If I lose mine honor,
I lose myself."* — William Shakespeare

SPIRITUAL PRINCIPLES

HONESTY

What is the spiritual principle of honesty?

Many belief systems and philosophies prioritize honesty, emphasizing the importance of truthfulness, authenticity, and integrity in our thoughts, words, and actions. It is rooted in the idea that living an honest life is not only a moral imperative but also a pathway to personal growth and spiritual enlightenment.

In essence, the principle of honesty involves being truthful with ourselves and others. It means having the courage to confront our own limitations, fears, and shortcomings, as well as acknowledging our strengths and virtues without denial or embellishment. Honesty in communication entails speaking the truth with kindness and compassion and avoiding falsehoods, exaggerations, or deceitful intentions. It encourages transparency in relationships, allowing us to connect on a deep and genuine level.

Moreover, the spiritual principle of honesty extends to our actions, emphasizing the importance of living a life that aligns with our inner values and moral principles. It involves behaving ethically, treating others with fairness and respect, and taking responsibility for our actions and their consequences. Honesty often requires self-examination and self-reflection, as we seek to understand our motivations and intentions. Ultimately, the spiritual principle of honesty serves as a guiding light on the journey toward self-realization, spiritual growth, and living in harmony with our beliefs and values.

How does honesty help recovery?

- **Self-awareness:** Honesty helps us recognize and accept our addiction. Admitting the truth about the extent and impact of addiction in our lives and the need for change is significant for recovery. It allows us to confront our behavior and take responsibility for our actions. Without honesty, it becomes difficult to recognize the severity of the problem and take the necessary steps toward recovery.

- **Overcoming denial:** Denial is a common defense mechanism in addiction. We may downplay the severity of our addiction, make excuses, or shift blame to others. Honesty helps us confront and break through this denial. By being honest about the extent of our addiction and its negative consequences, we can challenge our distorted thinking.

- **Accountability:** Honesty facilitates personal accountability. It enables us to take responsibility for our actions and choices. By being honest with ourselves and others, we can fully grasp the consequences of our addiction and the harm we may have inflicted on ourselves and others. By acknowledging our role in the addiction process, we take ownership of our actions and work toward making positive changes.

- **Building trust:** Addiction often leads to broken trust in relationships, as we may have lied, deceived, or manipulated others to support our unhealthy habits. Rebuilding trust is a vital aspect of recovery, and honesty is the key to achieving it. By consistently demonstrating honesty in words and actions, we can rebuild trust with loved ones, friends, and our broader support network. Trust provides a strong foundation for healthy relationships and ongoing support throughout our recovery journey.

- **Effective communication:** Open and honest communication is crucial in addiction recovery. It allows us to express our thoughts, emotions, and struggles effectively, making the necessary support and guidance possible. Honesty also facilitates productive conversations with healthcare professionals, therapists, and support groups, enabling tailored treatment plans and targeted interventions.

- **Identifying underlying issues:** Being honest about the underlying causes of addiction is vital for effective recovery. It requires us to explore and examine our emotions, experiences, and past traumas that may have contributed to our addiction. Honest self-reflection helps identify and address these root causes, paving the way for healing and growth.

- **Continued sobriety:** Maintaining long-term sobriety requires ongoing honesty. It involves being honest with ourselves about triggers, cravings, and potential relapse risks. Additionally, being honest about personal limitations and seeking help when needed is vital for avoiding relapse and maintaining a healthy recovery lifestyle.

What are ways to practice honesty?

- **Self-reflection:** Take time to reflect on your thoughts, actions, and feelings. Be honest with yourself about your past behaviors, mistakes, and challenges.

- **Open communication:** Share your struggles, progress, and feelings with a trusted friend, family member, or counselor. Openly discussing your journey can help you stay accountable and receive support.

- **Twelve-Step programs:** If you're part of a Twelve-Step program, like Alcoholics Anonymous or Narcotics Anonymous, honesty is a core principle. Regularly attend meetings and share your experiences with the group.

- **Admit mistakes:** Be willing to admit when you've made a mistake or have fallen off track. Acknowledging your shortcomings is a sign of strength and a step towards growth.

- 🌿 **Make amends:** As part of the recovery process, you may need to make amends to those you've hurt. Be honest about your past actions and apologize sincerely.

- 🌿 **Daily inventory:** Set aside time each day for self-examination. Reflect on your actions, emotions, and interactions, and be honest about areas where you can improve.

- 🌿 **Practice transparency:** Be open and honest with your support network about your triggers, cravings, and challenges. This helps others understand your needs and provide appropriate assistance.

- 🌿 **Avoid rationalizations:** Challenge any rationalizations or justifications for dishonest behavior. Be aware of any excuses you make to avoid facing the truth.

- 🌿 **Write in a journal:** Keeping a recovery journal can help you track your progress and express your thoughts and feelings honestly and without judgment.

- 🌿 **Mindful awareness:** Practice mindfulness to stay present in the moment. This can help you become more aware of your thoughts and behaviors, making it easier to be honest with yourself.

Honesty is fundamental to addiction recovery as it promotes self-awareness, personal accountability, trust-building, overcoming denial, effective communication, and long-term sobriety. By embracing honesty, we can confront our addiction, seek the necessary support, and develop healthier ways of thinking and behaving. This process of self-discovery and personal growth is essential for long-term recovery and a healthier, addiction-free life.

Remember, honesty is a journey, and it's okay to make mistakes along the way. The important thing is to continue striving for openness and truthfulness as part of your recovery process.

"Humility is the solid foundation of all virtues."
— Confucius

HUMILITY

What is the spiritual principle of humility?

Humility is a foundational concept in many religious and philosophical traditions. Humility is characterized by a humble and modest attitude, a willingness to acknowledge our limitations and imperfections, and a lack of arrogance or excessive pride. In a spiritual sense, it involves recognizing that there is something greater than ourselves, whether it's a higher power, a divine truth, or a sense of interconnectedness with all of creation.

Humility encourages us to approach life with a sense of openness, receptivity, and a readiness to learn and grow. It often goes hand in hand with virtues like gratitude, compassion, and service to others. Humility is seen as a path to deeper spiritual understanding, personal transformation, and harmonious relationships with others and the world. It's about surrendering the ego and embracing a more profound and selfless way of being in the world.

How does humility help recovery?

- **Acknowledging vulnerability:** Recovery begins with recognizing our vulnerability and the need for help. Humility enables us to admit that addiction has had a destructive impact on our lives and that we cannot overcome it on our own.

- **Openness to learning:** A humble attitude fosters a mindset of continuous learning and self-improvement. Those of us in recovery can benefit from new insights, strategies, and coping mechanisms to navigate life without substance abuse.

- **Accepting imperfections:** Humility encourages acceptance of our imperfections and past mistakes without judgment. It's about forgiving yourself for past actions and understanding that nobody is flawless.

- **Building authentic relationships:** In recovery, forming genuine connections with others is essential. Humility helps us engage in honest and empathetic relationships, free from the arrogance or defensiveness that can hinder communication.

- **Resisting relapse:** Recovery is an ongoing journey that may include relapses. A humble mindset allows us to admit our setbacks, seek support, and recommit to our sobriety goals rather than succumbing to denial or shame.

- **Developing gratitude:** Humility is closely tied to gratitude. Being grateful for the progress made and the support received in recovery reinforces a positive and optimistic outlook.

- **Surrendering control:** Addiction often thrives on the illusion of control. Humility involves surrendering the false belief that we can control everything and accepting that some aspects of life are beyond our control.

- **Connecting with a higher power:** For those with spiritual beliefs, humility plays a pivotal role in establishing a connection with a higher power. It involves recognizing that there is something greater than oneself that can provide guidance and strength.

What are ways to practice humility?

- **Self-reflection***:* Regularly engage in self-reflection to become aware of your thoughts, actions, and behaviors. Assess your strengths and weaknesses honestly.

- **Admit mistakes:** When you make a mistake or experience a setback, acknowledge it without blame or self-criticism. Accepting mistakes as opportunities for learning is a humble approach.

- **Seek feedback:** Encourage feedback from trusted friends, family members, or a sponsor. Be open to constructive criticism and use it as a tool for personal growth.

- **Practice gratitude:** Cultivate a sense of gratitude for the progress you've made in recovery and the support you've received. Regularly express thanks to those who have helped you.

- **Serve others:** Volunteer or engage in acts of service to help others in need. Selfless service is a powerful way to practice humility and connect with a greater purpose.

- **Maintain openness:** Stay open to different perspectives, especially when it comes to your recovery journey. Understand that there is no one-size-fits-all approach, and what works for others may not work for you.

- **Practice patience:** Patience is an essential element of humility. Recognize that personal growth and recovery take time, and progress may be slow at times.

- **Accept support:** Be willing to ask for help when needed, whether it's from a therapist, a support group, or a trusted friend. Acknowledging that you can't do it all on your own is a humble step.

- **Stay grounded:** Avoid letting success or progress in recovery inflate your ego. Remember where you came from and the challenges you've overcome to stay grounded.

- **Stay teachable**: Approach life with a "beginner's mind," a concept from Zen Buddhism, which means maintaining an attitude of openness, eagerness, and lack of preconceptions.

Humility serves as the cornerstone of recovery by fostering self-awareness, openness, authenticity, and resilience. It enables us to embrace our journey to sobriety with a genuine willingness to learn, grow, and seek support when needed. Remember that humility is a lifelong practice, and it's natural to have moments of ego or pride. The key is to recognize these moments and gently redirect yourself toward a humble mindset. Over time, humility becomes an integral part of our recovery journey, supporting our growth and well-being.

"Let your hopes, not your hurts, shape your future."
— Robert H. Schuller

HOPE

What is the spiritual principle of hope?

Hope is a positive and optimistic expectation for the future. It involves the belief that circumstances can improve and that positive outcomes are possible. Hope often involves trusting in a positive outcome despite current challenges. It is the belief that, no matter how difficult the present circumstances, there is a possibility for improvement. Hope is often linked to a sense of purpose or a higher meaning in life. It provides motivation and resilience by anchoring us to a broader perspective beyond immediate difficulties. In times of despair or hardship, hope serves as a guiding light. It offers solace and encouragement, helping us to persevere through challenges with the belief that things will get better. Hope empowers us to take positive actions toward our goals. It is a driving force behind efforts to overcome obstacles and work towards a better future.

How does hope help recovery?

- **Motivation for change:** Hope serves as a powerful motivator, inspiring us to make positive changes in our lives. It provides the energy and determination needed to overcome the challenges associated with recovery.

- **Positive outlook:** Hope fosters a positive outlook on the future. In the face of addiction, we may feel overwhelmed and hopeless. Embracing hope helps shift our perspective, allowing us to see a brighter and more optimistic outcome.

- **Resilience:** Recovery is often a challenging and nonlinear process. Hope enables us to bounce back from setbacks and challenges. It instills resilience, helping us persevere through difficulties without giving in to despair.

- **Belief in possibility:** Hope involves a belief in the possibility of change and improvement. It encourages us to envision a life free from the grip of addiction and to believe that recovery is achievable.

- **Empowerment:** Hope empowers us to take control of our lives. It promotes a sense of agency and personal responsibility, encouraging us to actively engage in the recovery process and make choices that align with our well-being.

- **Stress reduction:** Addiction and recovery come with stress and uncertainty. Hope serves as a buffer against stress by providing a sense of direction and purpose. It helps us navigate challenges with a more positive mindset.

- **Focus on solutions:** Hope shifts the focus from problems to solutions. Instead of dwelling on past mistakes or challenges, those of us with hope are more likely to seek and implement positive strategies for recovery.

- **Improved mental health:** The psychological benefits of hope include reduced feelings of helplessness and increased psychological well-being. Hope contributes to a more optimistic and resilient mindset, which is essential for maintaining mental health in recovery.

What are ways to apply hope?

- **Cultivate positive beliefs:** Actively work on cultivating positive beliefs about your recovery journey. Focus on the potential for growth, healing, and positive transformation. Recognize that setbacks are part of the process and not permanent roadblocks.

- **Set realistic goals:** Establish achievable short-term and long-term goals for your recovery. Break them down into smaller, manageable steps. Celebrate each milestone, as it reinforces the belief that change is possible.

- **Surround yourself with support:** Build a support network of individuals who share a positive and hopeful outlook. Engage with friends, family, or members of a recovery community who uplift and inspire you. Connections with others on a similar journey can be a powerful source of hope.

- **Practice mindfulness:** Incorporate mindfulness practices into your daily routine. Mindfulness encourages staying present in the moment and letting go of negative thoughts about the past or worries about the future. This practice fosters a sense of peace and hope in the current moment.

- **Seek professional guidance:** Engage with therapists, counselors, or mentors who can provide professional guidance. They can offer insights, coping strategies, and encouragement, reinforcing belief in the possibility of positive change.

- **Celebrate progress:** Acknowledge and celebrate your achievements, no matter how small. Reflecting on your progress reinforces the idea that change is happening, and it bolsters the hope for continued growth.

- **Engage in inspirational activities:** Surround yourself with inspirational content. This could include reading books, listening to podcasts, or watching videos that share stories of recovery, resilience, and transformation. Inspirational content can serve as a daily reminder of the potential for positive change.

- **Visualize your future:** Spend time visualizing a future that aligns with your recovery goals. Envision the positive aspects of a sober and fulfilling life. This visualization can serve as a powerful motivator and instill hope for the journey ahead.

- **Practice gratitude:** Regularly express gratitude for the positive aspects of your life. Gratitude shifts the focus from what is lacking to what is present, fostering a sense of contentment and hope.

🌿 **Embrace a spiritual practice:** For those with spiritual beliefs, engaging in practices such as prayer or meditation can provide a sense of connection to a higher power and reinforce the belief that you are not alone on your journey.

The principle of hope is dynamic and can be nurtured and strengthened over time. Consistent effort and a willingness to embrace positive change contribute to a hopeful outlook on the recovery journey. Having hope is not only a beacon of light but also a driving force that propels us forward, helping us to overcome obstacles and build a meaningful life beyond addiction.

"Courage doesn't always roar. Sometimes courage is the quiet voice at the end of the day saying, 'I will try again tomorrow.'" — Mary Anne Radmacher

COURAGE

What is the spiritual principle of courage?

Courage refers to the inner strength and bravery to face challenges, adversity, and fears in life while remaining true to our values and convictions. It involves the willingness to take risks, step out of our comfort zone, and confront obstacles, even when the path ahead is uncertain or difficult.

In a spiritual context, courage is often associated with moral and ethical fortitude. It means standing up for what is right and just, even when it's unpopular or personally challenging. It can also involve the courage to confront our own limitations, fears, and egos as part of a journey toward personal growth and spiritual development.

Practicing courage in a spiritual sense may involve acts of integrity, honesty, and compassion, especially when they require personal sacrifice or vulnerability. It can also entail facing our inner demons, such as negative thought patterns or past traumas, with the goal of healing and transformation.

Overall, the spiritual principle of courage is about aligning one's actions and choices with higher values and purposes, even in the face of difficulty or resistance, and it is often seen as an essential aspect of spiritual and personal development.

How does courage help recovery?

- **Facing addiction:** Recovery often begins with the courage to admit our addiction and the need for help. It takes immense courage to confront our own weaknesses and acknowledge the impact of addiction on our life.

- **Overcoming fear:** Many of us in recovery face fears related to withdrawal, change, or the unknown path ahead. Courage is necessary to confront these fears and move forward with the recovery process.

- **Rebuilding relationships:** Addiction can strain or damage relationships. Courage is needed to repair these connections, often involving difficult conversations and apologies.

- **Embracing change:** Recovery entails significant life changes, including adopting healthier habits, building new relationships, and letting go of old patterns. Courage is essential to embrace and navigate these changes.

- **Seeking support:** It takes courage to reach out for help, whether through therapy, support groups, or talking to loved ones about our struggles. This support is vital in the recovery journey.

- **Self-reflection:** Recovery often involves deep self-reflection to understand the underlying causes of addiction. Having the courage to explore our past and confront difficult emotions is an essential part of healing.

- **Building resilience:** Courage helps us build resilience to cope with life's challenges without turning to addictive behaviors. It enables us to face setbacks and disappointments without giving up on our recovery.

- **Building self-esteem:** Many individuals in recovery have low self-esteem due to their past actions. Having the courage to work on self-improvement and self-acceptance is crucial.

- **Empowering growth:** Courage empowers those of us in recovery to set goals, pursue personal growth, and work toward a fulfilling life beyond addiction.

- **Inspiring others:** Demonstrating courage in recovery can inspire others who are struggling with addiction. By sharing your journey, you can provide hope and encouragement to those seeking help.

What are ways to embrace courage?

- **Acknowledge your fears:** Begin by recognizing and accepting the fears that may be holding you back in your recovery. This might include the fear of facing past mistakes, the fear of change, or the fear of relapse. Understanding these fears is the first step in overcoming them.

- **Set small goals:** Break your recovery journey into smaller, manageable goals. This makes it easier to take courageous steps, one at a time. Each small success builds confidence and courage for the next step.

- **Take responsibility:** Courage involves taking responsibility for our actions and decisions. Acknowledge the impact of your addiction on your life and those around you. Accepting responsibility is a brave step toward making amends.

- **Embrace change:** Understand that change is a part of recovery. Embrace it as an opportunity for growth and healing. The courage to let go of old habits and embrace new ones is key to long-term recovery.

- **Face your triggers:** Identify the people, places, or situations that trigger cravings or temptations. Confront these triggers with a plan for how to respond courageously, such as by reaching out to a sponsor or engaging in a healthy alternative activity.

- **Help others**: Sharing your own experiences and providing support to others in recovery can be a courageous and fulfilling act. It not only helps them but also reinforces your commitment to recovery.

- 🖋 **Admit your struggles:** The first step in recovery is acknowledging your addiction and the challenges you face. Admitting the problem takes courage, but it's essential for moving forward.

- 🖋 **Seek professional help***: Asking for professional help takes courage and is a significant step toward recovery. Courage helps us trust in the process of recovery and treatment programs and receive what we need for long-term sobriety.

- 🖋 **Stay committed:** Recovery is a long-term process, and there may be setbacks. Staying committed and getting back on track after a relapse requires courage and resilience.

Courage is vital in recovery as it empowers us to confront addiction, overcome fear, make amends, embrace change, seek support, reflect on ourselves, build resilience, empower growth, and inspire others. Courage is not the absence of fear but the determination to keep moving forward despite it. Recovery is a courageous journey, and every step you take toward healing is a testament to your strength and determination.

"Faith is taking the first step even when you don't see the whole staircase." — Martin Luther King Jr.

FAITH

What is the spiritual principle of faith?

Faith is a foundational belief characterized by a profound trust, an unwavering confidence, and a deep conviction in something that may not be immediately verifiable or apparent. Its interpretations can vary across different contexts. In religious settings, faith often pertains to a steadfast belief in a higher power, religious doctrines, and spiritual truths. Alternatively, spiritual faith may encompass a broader belief in higher consciousness and the interconnectedness of all living things. On a personal level, having faith in oneself involves trusting in one's capabilities to overcome challenges. Faith in others underscores trust in the integrity and goodwill of individuals, forming a basis for healthy relationships. Furthermore, faith can extend to an optimistic outlook on the future and a belief in positive outcomes.

Additionally, people may exhibit faith in guiding principles, values, or ethical standards that shape their decisions and actions. Ultimately, the principle of faith often involves embracing certain truths or beliefs without empirical evidence. It serves as a source of motivation, guidance, and resilience across various facets of life.

How does faith help recovery?

- **Source of strength and resilience**: Faith can provide a deep well of inner strength, helping us to endure the challenges of recovery with resilience. Believing in a higher power or a greater purpose can offer a sense of support during difficult times.

- **Hope and optimism:** Faith instills hope and optimism for the future. Whether it's faith in a higher power, the recovery process, or personal growth, maintaining a positive outlook can be a powerful motivator for those of us navigating the complexities of recovery.

- **Meaning and purpose:** Faith often provides us with a sense of meaning and purpose. Believing in something beyond addiction can give life a greater sense of direction and significance, motivating us to stay committed to our recovery journey.

- **Community and support:** Many faith traditions emphasize community and support networks. Being part of a faith community or having spiritual connections can provide a sense of belonging, understanding, and encouragement during the recovery process.

- **Coping mechanism:** Faith can serve as a coping mechanism, helping us to deal with our pain, fear, and loss. Having faith in a higher power or a greater plan can help to alleviate the burden of these feelings, providing a sense of relief and comfort.

What are ways to cultivate faith?

- **Set realistic goals:** Establish achievable short-term and long-term goals for your recovery. Celebrate your progress as you work toward these goals, reinforcing your faith in your ability to change.

- **Surround yourself with positive influences:** Build a supportive network of friends, family, or a recovery community. Positive relationships can provide encouragement and reinforce your faith in the recovery process.

- **Practice mindfulness:** Engage in mindfulness meditation or other mindfulness practices. Being present in the moment can help you manage stress, cravings, and negative thoughts, fostering a deeper sense of faith in your ability to stay sober.

- **Educate yourself:** Learn about addiction, recovery strategies, and the science behind behavioral change. Knowledge empowers you to make informed decisions and can boost your faith in the effectiveness of recovery methods.

- **Maintain a journal:** Keep a journal to document your thoughts, feelings, and progress in recovery. Reflecting on your journey can reinforce your faith in personal growth and change.

- **Practice gratitude:** Cultivate a habit of gratitude by regularly acknowledging the positive aspects of your life. Recognizing the good can help shift your perspective and bolster your faith in a brighter future.

- **Engage in physical activity:** Incorporate regular exercise into your routine. Physical activity can improve mood, reduce stress, and enhance overall well-being, contributing to your faith in a healthier lifestyle.

- **Stay connected to your values:** Reflect on your personal values and principles. Align your actions with these values, reinforcing your faith in living a life consistent with your beliefs.

- **Visualize success:** Use visualization techniques to imagine a positive and successful future in recovery. Creating mental images of your desired outcomes can reinforce your faith in achieving them.

- **Stay committed:** Recognize that setbacks are a natural part of recovery. Maintain your commitment to the journey, knowing that each day is an opportunity to reinforce your faith in lasting change.

It's essential to recognize that the role of faith in recovery is subjective and varies among individuals. Some may find profound support in religious or spiritual beliefs, while others may draw strength from a broader sense of faith in themselves, their support systems, or the recovery process. Additionally, faith can complement evidence-based treatments and counseling in a comprehensive approach to recovery. Remember that cultivating faith is a personal and ongoing process. Be patient with yourself and embrace the gradual unfolding of positive change in your life.

"To forgive is to set a prisoner free and discover that the prisoner was you." — Lewis B. Smedes

FORGIVENESS

What is the spiritual principle of forgiveness?

Forgiveness is a fundamental concept found in many religious and philosophical traditions. At its core, forgiveness involves letting go of negative emotions such as resentment, anger, or the desire for revenge towards someone who has wronged us. It goes beyond simply excusing or condoning harmful actions; instead, it is a deeply personal and often transformative process of healing and reconciliation.

Forgiveness is rooted in the idea of extending compassion and mercy, both to others and to ourselves. It is the acknowledgment of the human capacity for making mistakes and realization that holding onto grudges and anger can be detrimental to one's own well-being. By forgiving, we free ourselves from the burden of carrying emotional wounds and find a path to inner peace and emotional healing.

Moreover, forgiveness is often seen as a spiritual practice that aligns with higher values and principles. In many spiritual traditions, forgiveness is regarded as an act of grace and a reflection of divine love and mercy. It is seen as a way to transcend ego-driven emotions and connect with a higher, more compassionate aspect of ourselves.

Overall, the spiritual principle of forgiveness emphasizes the transformative power of compassion, letting go of the past, and fostering inner and outer reconciliation. It is a profound concept that holds the potential for healing, personal growth, and spiritual development.

How does forgiveness help in recovery?

- **Healing from past trauma:** Many of us have experienced significant trauma, whether related to our addiction or other life events. Forgiveness allows us to release the emotional pain and trauma associated with past wrongs, facilitating the healing process. It's a crucial step in addressing the root causes of addiction.

- **Breaking the cycle:** Addiction often involves cycles of blame, guilt, and resentment. These negative emotions can perpetuate addictive behaviors. Forgiveness interrupts this cycle by replacing resentment with compassion and self-compassion, paving the way for healthier emotional responses.

- **Rebuilding relationships:** Addiction can strain or sever relationships with loved ones. Forgiveness, both of ourselves and others, can be instrumental in rebuilding these connections. It fosters understanding, empathy, and the opportunity for reconciliation, supporting a strong and sober support system.

- **Releasing emotional weight:** Carrying grudges and resentment can be emotionally exhausting and detrimental to mental health. Forgiveness lightens this emotional burden, reducing stress and promoting overall well-being. It's an essential aspect of emotional sobriety.

- **Promoting self-acceptance:** In recovery, we often confront shame and guilt related to past actions. Forgiving ourselves is an act of self-acceptance and self-compassion. It allows us to move forward with a sense of worthiness and self-love, which are essential for maintaining sobriety.

- **Spiritual growth:** Forgiveness aligns with many spiritual principles, emphasizing compassion, love, and the importance of letting go of ego-driven emotions. Engaging in forgiveness practices can deepen our spiritual connection and provide a sense of purpose and meaning in recovery.

- **Reducing relapse risk:** Negative emotions like anger, guilt, and resentment can trigger relapse. Forgiveness helps manage these triggers, reducing the likelihood of returning to addictive behaviors during challenging moments.

- **Embracing personal responsibility:** Recovery involves taking responsibility for our actions and choices. Forgiveness allows us to acknowledge our past mistakes without judgment and take proactive steps toward positive change.

- **Inner peace:** Ultimately, forgiveness leads to a sense of inner peace. It allows us to let go of the past and focus on the present and future, promoting emotional stability and resilience.

What are ways to practice forgiveness?

- **Self-forgiveness:** Begin by forgiving yourself for past mistakes and transgressions related to you personally, as well as for your addiction. You are not defined by your past actions, including your addiction. Practice self-compassion and treat yourself with the same kindness you would offer to a friend.

- **Identify resentments:** Make a list of people or situations you hold resentment towards. These could be individuals who contributed to your addiction or those you blame for past pain. Identifying these resentments is the first step toward forgiveness.

- **Acknowledge feelings:** It's essential to acknowledge and process your feelings related to resentments. Allow yourself to feel anger, hurt, or sadness without judgment. Journaling or talking to a therapist or support group can be helpful.

- **Understand their perspective:** Try to see the situation from the perspective of the person you resent. This doesn't mean condoning their actions, but rather gaining insight into their motivations and circumstances. Understanding can lead to empathy.

- **Practice empathy:** Cultivate empathy for yourself and others. Recognize that everyone is human and makes mistakes. Empathy is a powerful tool for breaking down barriers to forgiveness.

- **Make amends:** When you are ready and it won't harm yourself or others, make amends to those you've wronged in a thoughtful and sincere manner.

- **Letting go:** Forgiveness is about letting go of the desire for revenge or retribution. It doesn't mean forgetting the past, but it does mean choosing not to be controlled by it. Visualize releasing the negative emotions associated with your resentments.

- **Letting go rituals:** Consider symbolic acts of letting go, like writing your resentments on paper and then burning or burying them, as a way to physically release negative feelings.

- **Reflect on the benefits:** Consider the positive effects of forgiveness on your mental and emotional well-being. Remember that forgiveness is a gift you give to yourself, as it frees you from the burden of resentment and anger.

- **Seek support:** Forgiveness can be a challenging process. Seek support from a therapist, counselor, or recovery support group. Sharing your experiences and challenges with others who have gone through similar journeys can be immensely beneficial.

Forgiveness is a cornerstone of recovery that empowers us to transform our lives and find lasting sobriety and well-being. Learning to practice forgiveness is a personal journey, and there is no set timeline. It's okay if it takes time to fully forgive and let go of resentments. The goal is to free yourself from the burden of negative emotions, promote healing, and create a healthier, more fulfilling life in recovery.

"Gratitude is a divine attitude in the wisdom traditions. It takes you out from the ego self and takes you into the higher self. That higher state of consciousness initiates self-repair, self-regulation and healing." — Deepak Chopra

GRATITUDE

What is the spiritual principle of gratitude?

Gratitude involves intentionally focusing on and appreciating the positive aspects of our lives, experiences, and surroundings. It's about acknowledging and valuing the things we have, the people around us, and the circumstances that contribute to our well-being and happiness. Gratitude is a mindset that encourages us to recognize the good, even amidst challenges and difficulties. In a spiritual context, gratitude is often seen as a powerful practice that can bring about a shift in perspective, leading to increased happiness, contentment, and a sense of abundance. It encourages us to focus on what we have rather than what we lack, fostering a greater sense of positivity and inner peace.

Practicing gratitude is considered a transformative tool that can lead to spiritual growth and emotional healing. It helps us let go of negative emotions and attitudes, such as resentment and envy, by redirecting our attention to the positive aspects of life. Gratitude is also seen as a way to deepen our connection with a higher power, as it reflects a recognition of the gifts provided by the universe.

Overall, gratitude involves a mindful and intentional shift in perspective towards acknowledging and appreciating the abundance and beauty present in our lives, leading to a more fulfilling and spiritually aligned existence.

How does gratitude help recovery?

- **Shifts focus:** Recovery often involves facing challenges and addressing past mistakes. Gratitude shifts the focus from dwelling on difficulties to appreciating the progress made and the positive aspects of life, fostering a more optimistic outlook.

- **Mindset change:** Gratitude encourages a shift from a mindset of lack to one of abundance. This change in perspective can help us appreciate the blessings we have, which can be instrumental in combating feelings of emptiness that may have contributed to addictive behaviors.

- **Cultivates positivity:** Practicing gratitude promotes a positive mindset, which is essential for maintaining motivation and resilience during recovery. It helps us focus on the progress we've made rather than fixating on setbacks.

- **Enhances emotional well-being:** Gratitude has been linked to improved emotional well-being. It can help reduce feelings of depression, anxiety, and stress often experienced during recovery, leading to a more stable and balanced emotional state.

- **Promotes humility:** Gratitude fosters humility by acknowledging the support and resources received from others. This humility can counteract the ego-driven behaviors that might have fueled addiction.

- **Counteracts self-pity:** Addiction can lead to feelings of self-pity and victimization. Gratitude encourages us to take responsibility for our actions and focus on the opportunities for growth and positive change.

- **Strengthens resilience:** Recovery is a journey that includes ups and downs. Gratitude strengthens the capacity to cope with challenges, setbacks, and triggers, enhancing resilience and the ability to navigate tough times.

- **Enhances relationships:** Expressing gratitude toward others, especially those who have supported the recovery process, strengthens relationships and builds a sense of community, providing a vital support network.

- **Connection to higher power:** Gratitude is often intertwined with spirituality. Expressing gratitude fosters a deeper connection to a higher power or the universe, enhancing the spiritual aspect of recovery.

- **Prevents relapse:** Cultivating a mindset of gratitude can reduce the inclination to return to addictive behaviors as we become more invested in maintaining our progress and positive changes.

What are ways to practice gratitude?

- **Gratitude journal:** Set aside time each day to write down three to five things you're grateful for. This practice helps you focus on the positive aspects of your life and encourages reflection.

- **Morning ritual:** Begin your day by expressing gratitude for the opportunities and experiences that lie ahead. This can set a positive tone for the rest of the day.

- **Mindful moments:** Throughout your day, pause to acknowledge and appreciate the little things around you, whether it's a beautiful sunrise, a kind gesture, or a moment of peace.

- **Gratitude meditation:** Incorporate a gratitude meditation into your routine. During this practice, reflect on the things you're grateful for and allow the feelings of gratitude to come forward.

- **Gratitude letters:** Write letters of gratitude to people who have positively impacted your life. You can choose to send these letters or keep them as a personal reflection.

- ✍ **Express appreciation**: Verbalize your gratitude to friends, family, and those who have supported you in your recovery journey. A simple "thank you" can go a long way.

- ✍ **Daily affirmations:** Incorporate gratitude into your daily affirmations. Repeat positive statements about the things you're thankful for to reinforce your mindset.

- ✍ **Practice non-comparative gratitude:** Instead of comparing your situation to others', focus on what you have, regardless of how it compares to someone else's circumstances.

- ✍ **Pause before meals:** Take a moment before each meal to express gratitude for the nourishment you're about to receive.

- ✍ **Evening reflection:** Before bed, reflect on the day and identify moments that brought you joy, contentment, or a sense of gratitude.

The practice of gratitude has been linked to numerous psychological and emotional benefits. It can lead to increased feelings of happiness, reduced stress, improved relationships, enhanced resilience, and an overall more positive outlook on life. Over time, it can reshape our outlook, helping us appreciate the positives in our lives, no matter how small, and contributing to our overall well-being. In essence, the practice of gratitude serves as a powerful tool in recovery, fostering a positive and transformative mindset that supports emotional, psychological, and spiritual healing.

"Our sorrows and wounds are healed only when we touch them with compassion." — Jack Kornfield

COMPASSION

What is the spiritual principle of compassion?

Compassion is a profound concept emphasizing deep empathy, understanding, and kindness toward ourselves and others. It forms the cornerstone of various spiritual and religious traditions, promoting core human virtues. Compassion begins with empathy, which is the ability to genuinely comprehend and share the emotions and experiences of others. It manifests in acts of kindness and care, where we reach out to offer support, love, and assistance without expecting anything in return. Central to compassion is the practice of suspending judgment and accepting people as they are, acknowledging that everyone faces their own unique challenges and imperfections. Forgiveness is another integral element, encouraging us to release anger and resentment and realize that clinging to negative emotions harms both the person holding them and their target. Furthermore, compassion extends mercy and aid to those in suffering or adversity, even when it may not be anticipated or warranted.

Compassion underscores the interconnectedness of all living beings, emphasizing that our actions have a ripple effect on others and the world at large. A crucial facet is self-compassion, which reminds us to treat ourselves with the same empathy and kindness we extend to others. This self-compassion is vital for personal well-being, as it acknowledges that self-criticism and judgment can be detrimental. In essence, the spiritual principle of compassion encourages us to nurture a heart-centered and caring attitude, fostering a world where people interact with kindness, respect, and understanding while recognizing the intrinsic worth and dignity of every individual.

How does compassion help recovery?

- **Self-compassion:** Compassion starts with ourselves. We often carry feelings of guilt, shame, and self-judgment due to our past actions during addiction. Practicing self-compassion involves treating ourselves with the same kindness and understanding that one would offer to a friend. It helps in healing emotional wounds, reducing self-criticism, and fostering self-acceptance.

- **Empathy for others:** Compassion allows us to empathize with others who may be going through similar challenges. This empathy can lead to deeper and more meaningful connections with our fellows in recovery, providing a sense of belonging and support within a recovery community.

- **Forgiveness:** Compassion can lead to forgiveness, both for ourselves and for others who may have contributed to past pain or trauma. Letting go of resentment and grudges is essential for emotional healing and personal growth in recovery.

- **Reducing isolation:** Addiction often leads to isolation and disconnection from loved ones. Compassion encourages reaching out to mend broken relationships, offering apologies where needed, and rebuilding connections with family and friends.

- **Motivation for recovery:** Compassion can be a powerful motivator for staying committed to the recovery journey. When we genuinely care for our own well-being and the well-being of others, we are more likely to make choices that support our sobriety and overall health.

- **Stress reduction:** Compassion practices, such as mindfulness meditation or loving-kindness meditation, can reduce stress and anxiety, which are common triggers for relapse. These practices promote emotional regulation and resilience in the face of life's challenges.

- **Altruism:** Engaging in acts of compassion and service to others, such as volunteering or helping our fellows in recovery, can provide a sense of purpose and fulfillment, contributing to our overall well-being and recovery.

- **Spiritual growth:** Many spiritual and religious traditions emphasize the importance of compassion as a path to spiritual growth. Embracing this principle can lead to a deeper sense of connection to a higher power or spiritual dimension, providing strength and guidance in recovery.

What are ways to practice compassion?

- **Self-compassion:** Begin by showing compassion to yourself. Treat yourself with the same kindness, understanding, and forgiveness that you would offer to a friend who is going through a challenging time. When you make a mistake or face setbacks in recovery, practice self-compassion by acknowledging your imperfections without self-criticism.

- **Mindfulness meditation:** Mindfulness meditation helps you become aware of your thoughts and emotions without judgment. Through mindfulness, you can observe your own suffering and pain with compassion. This practice can help you better understand your feelings and respond to them with greater self-compassion.

- **Loving-kindness meditation:** This meditation practice involves generating feelings of love and compassion toward yourself and others. Start by offering phrases like "May I be happy, may I be healthy, may I be free from suffering," and then extend these wishes to loved ones, acquaintances, and even those you have conflicts with. This practice helps cultivate feelings of compassion and empathy.

- **Practice empathy:** Make an effort to understand and empathize with the experiences and challenges of others, especially those who are also in recovery. Active listening and offering support can go a long way in demonstrating compassion.

- 🌿 **Compassionate self-talk:** Pay attention to your self-talk and replace self-criticism with self-compassion. Instead of berating yourself for mistakes and setbacks, acknowledge your efforts and treat yourself with words of understanding and encouragement.

- 🌿 **Volunteer or help others:** Engaging in acts of kindness and service can be a practical way to practice compassion. Consider volunteering for a charitable organization or offering support to fellow recovering individuals. These actions not only help others but also foster a sense of purpose and fulfillment in your own life.

- 🌿 **Forgiveness:** Work on forgiving yourself and others for past mistakes and wrongdoings. Holding onto grudges and resentment can block the flow of compassion. Forgiveness is a compassionate act that can lead to emotional healing.

- 🌿 **Join a support group:** Participating in a recovery support group can provide a sense of community and understanding. Sharing your experiences and listening to others can foster compassion for both yourself and fellow group members.

- 🌿 **Practice patience:** Recovery is a journey, and it may involve setbacks and relapses. Practice patience with yourself during these times, knowing that healing and progress take time.

- 🌿 **Reflect on compassion:** Regularly take time to reflect on the concept of compassion, its importance in your recovery, and how you can continue to cultivate it in your life. Journaling about your experiences and insights can be helpful.

Practicing compassion in recovery is a powerful way to promote healing, personal growth, and positive relationships. It's an ongoing process, and it may take time to develop this skill. Be patient with yourself as you integrate compassion into your recovery journey, and recognize that it can be a powerful tool for personal transformation and healing. Over time, consistent practice can lead to increased compassion, emotional healing, and more meaningful connections with others.

"Acceptance is not submission; it is acknowledgment of the facts of a situation, recognition of a condition." — E. W. Howe

ACCEPTANCE

What is the spiritual principle of acceptance?

Acceptance is about recognizing and embracing the way things are in life without trying to judge, fight, or change them. It's making peace with both the good and not-so-good parts of life, whether they're happening outside you (in the world) or inside you (your feelings and thoughts). Many spiritual and philosophical beliefs see acceptance as a key step toward finding inner calm, growing as a person, and gaining spiritual wisdom.

Acceptance doesn't mean just giving up or agreeing with everything, especially when things aren't going well. Instead, it's about honestly seeing a situation for what it is and deciding how you want to deal with it in a way that matches your values and keeps you peaceful. It's letting go of the need to control everything or insisting that life should be different, which often leads to more problems. Instead, acceptance helps you be in the present moment, open to whatever comes your way, and find strength in accepting what can't be changed.

For those of us in recovery, acceptance can be extremely beneficial. It means facing up to the reality of addiction, understanding how it's been hurting you, and agreeing that it's time for change and healing. It's also about accepting yourself, including your mistakes and imperfections, and deciding to take the path of recovery with kindness towards yourself. In the end, acceptance brings inner peace, resilience, and the skill to handle the ups and downs of life with a calm and steady heart.

How does acceptance help recovery?

- **Reduced stress and anxiety:** Acceptance helps us let go of the constant struggle against reality, which can be a significant source of stress and anxiety. Instead of resisting what is, we learn to go with the flow and find peace in the present moment.

- **Improved emotional well-being:** Acceptance allows us to acknowledge our emotions without judgment. This self-compassion and emotional honesty can lead to better mental health and a reduction in negative emotional states like guilt, shame, and anger.

- **Stronger resilience:** Acceptance teaches resilience by helping us adapt to life's challenges more effectively. When we accept that setbacks are a part of life, we can bounce back quicker and with more strength.

- **Enhanced relationships:** Acceptance extends to people and their imperfections, which can lead to more harmonious relationships. By accepting others as they are, we can reduce conflict and build deeper connections.

- **Greater self-awareness:** Acceptance encourages introspection and self-awareness. It allows us to see our strengths and weaknesses clearly, which is essential for personal growth and making positive changes.

- **Reduced relapse risk:** Acceptance plays a crucial role in addiction recovery. Accepting the reality of addiction and its consequences is the first step toward healing and sobriety. It helps us commit to the recovery journey with determination.

- **Improved problem-solving:** Instead of dwelling on problems, acceptance encourages us to focus on solutions. It frees up mental energy that can be channeled into finding constructive ways to address challenges.

- **Enhanced spirituality:** Many spiritual paths emphasize acceptance as a way to connect with a higher power or the universe. It fosters a sense of peace and pathway through the spiritual journey.

- **Increased mindfulness:** Acceptance is closely tied to mindfulness, the practice of being fully present in the moment. Mindfulness can help us stay grounded and make healthier choices.

- **Personal freedom:** Ultimately, acceptance leads to a sense of inner freedom. It liberates us from the need to control everything and allows us to live more authentically and peacefully.

What are ways to practice acceptance?

- **Mindfulness meditation:** Engage in mindfulness meditation to bring awareness to the present moment without judgment. This practice enhances the ability to accept things as they are.

- **Radical acceptance:** Embrace the concept of radical acceptance, acknowledging that some things are beyond your control and that resisting them only leads to suffering.

- **Daily affirmations:** Use positive affirmations to reinforce self-acceptance and affirm your commitment to the recovery journey.

- **Journaling:** Keep a recovery journal to reflect on your experiences, emotions, and progress. This can help in accepting the ups and downs of the journey.

- **Yoga practices:** Incorporate yoga practices that focus on acceptance and self-compassion. Yoga can be a holistic approach to physical and mental well-being.

- **Attend acceptance-based therapy:** Explore therapies like Acceptance and Commitment Therapy (ACT), which specifically targets acceptance as a core component.

- **Educate yourself:** Learn about the nature of addiction, recovery processes, and the science behind it. Education can empower you to accept the realities of the journey.

- **Letting go of resentments:** Work on letting go of resentments and grievances from the past. Acceptance involves releasing the emotional burden of past experiences.

- **Stay present:** Focus on the present moment rather than dwelling on the past or worrying about the future. Acceptance thrives in the here and now.

- **Nature connection:** Spend time in nature, contemplating the cycles of growth, change, and acceptance observed in the natural world.

Practicing acceptance is a transformative process that can significantly benefit us by improving our emotional well-being, relationships, resilience, self-awareness, and overall quality of life. Remember, acceptance is an ongoing practice, and progress may come in small steps. It's about developing a mindset that embraces the journey of recovery, including its challenges and victories, as well as finding lasting healing and inner peace.

> *"Peace requires us to surrender our illusions of control."* — Jack Kornfield

SURRENDER

What is the spiritual principle of surrender?

Surrender involves letting go of the need for control, releasing resistance, and accepting the flow of life as it unfolds. It is often associated with trust in a higher power or a divine order, recognizing that there are aspects of existence beyond our control. Surrendering in a spiritual context means relinquishing our ego-driven desires and allowing things to happen naturally, with faith that there is a greater plan or purpose at work. This principle encourages us to be present in the moment, to accept the truth of our circumstances, and to find inner peace in the act of surrender.

Surrender is not passive resignation; it's an active choice to stop fighting against the current of life and to align yourself with the greater forces of the universe. It involves a profound level of trust and a willingness to release attachments to specific outcomes. Surrender is often considered a path to spiritual growth, personal transformation, and a deeper connection to the mysteries of existence. It can bring about a sense of freedom, relief from anxiety, and a greater capacity to cope with life's challenges.

How does surrender help recovery?

- **Letting go of control:** Surrender involves releasing the illusion of control over our lives. In recovery, admitting powerlessness over addiction and acknowledging the inability to control every aspect of life is a transformative step. It allows us to relinquish the burdens of constant self-management.

- **Acceptance of reality:** Surrender encourages the acceptance of reality as it is, without resistance. This acceptance is crucial in recovery, as it involves acknowledging the impact of addiction, understanding the need for change, and facing the challenges of the healing process with openness.

- **Connection to a higher power:** Surrender often involves connecting to a higher power or a force beyond our understanding. In recovery, this connection becomes a source of strength and guidance. It provides a sense of support, comfort, and purpose, helping individuals navigate the complexities of the recovery journey.

- **Release of shame and guilt:** Surrendering involves letting go of the heavy burden of shame and guilt associated with addiction. It allows us to forgive ourselves, recognize our vulnerabilities, and move forward with self-compassion.

- **Embracing help:** Surrender is synonymous with seeking help. In recovery, it means acknowledging the need for support from others, whether through therapy, support groups, or spiritual guidance. It fosters a sense of community and shared understanding.

- **Transformative healing:** Surrender is a catalyst for transformative healing. By surrendering to the recovery process, we open ourselves to personal growth, emotional healing, and a renewed sense of purpose.

- **Reducing resistance:** Surrendering reduces resistance to change. In recovery, it allows us to embrace new ways of thinking and living without the resistance that often hinders progress.

- **Living in the present:** Surrender encourages living in the present moment, focusing on the now rather than dwelling on past mistakes or fearing the future. This mindfulness is a valuable skill in recovery.

What are ways to surrender?

- ☙ **Admitting powerlessness:** Acknowledge the inability to control addictive behaviors and accept that they have become unmanageable. This is the first step in surrendering to the reality of addiction.

- ☙ **Seeking help:** Surrendering involves reaching out for support. This could mean seeking professional help, joining a support group, or confiding in friends and family. It's a recognition that overcoming addiction requires collaboration and assistance.

- ☙ **Embracing a higher power:** For those with a spiritual or religious inclination, surrender often involves acknowledging a higher power. This might be through prayer, meditation, or any practice that fosters a connection to something beyond oneself.

- ☙ **Letting go of resentments:** Holding onto resentments and grudges can hinder recovery. Surrendering means letting go of these negative emotions, forgiving oneself and others, and focusing on the present.

- ☙ **Living one day at a time:** Instead of getting overwhelmed by the prospect of a lifelong recovery journey, surrendering involves taking it one day at a time. Focus on the present moment and the actions needed for today's sobriety.

- ☙ **Openness to change:** Surrendering requires an openness to change. This might involve adopting new habits, letting go of old patterns, and being willing to explore different ways of thinking and living.

- ☙ **Acceptance of imperfection***:* Surrendering involves accepting one's imperfections and limitations. It means recognizing that recovery is a process that and there will be setbacks along the way.

- **Mindfulness and meditation:** Practices like mindfulness and meditation can help in surrendering to the present moment. These practices cultivate awareness, reduce anxiety about the future, and promote a sense of calm.

- **Participating in a recovery community:** Being part of a recovery community provides a sense of connection and shared experience. It involves surrendering the idea of going through recovery alone and embracing the support of others.

- **Continued learning:** Surrendering involves recognizing that there is always more to learn. This might include attending workshops, reading recovery literature, or engaging in activities that promote personal growth.

In the context of recovery, surrender plays a pivotal role. It involves acknowledging one's powerlessness over addiction, admitting the need for help, and relinquishing the illusion of control. Surrender is a transformative process that opens the door to healing, growth, and a deeper connection to a source of support and guidance beyond oneself. Embracing the principle of surrender in recovery is often seen as a crucial step toward lasting sobriety and spiritual well-being.

> *"The willingness to grow is the essence of all spiritual development."* — Bill W.

WILLINGNESS

What is the spiritual principle of willingness?

Willingness holds a central place in the process of recovery and personal development. It signifies our readiness and enthusiasm for taking action, making substantial changes, and embracing new experiences, particularly in the context of conquering addiction or facing life's challenges. Willingness forms the solid foundation on which recovery stands because it embodies a sincere desire for transformation and the creation of positive change. This principle encompasses several key aspects, such as being open to change, actively participating in the recovery journey, facing challenges with determination, surrendering control over negative behaviors, taking responsibility for our actions, maintaining a positive attitude, seeking and embracing support, and viewing experiences, even setbacks, as opportunities for learning and growth. In summary, willingness serves as the driving force that motivates us to embark on the path of recovery and personal growth, symbolizing our dedication to self-improvement and the pursuit of a more fulfilling life.

How does willingness help recovery?

- **Openness to change:** Recovery often necessitates significant life changes, such as giving up substance use, adopting healthier behaviors, and addressing past traumas. Willingness enables us to be open to these changes, even when they may be difficult or uncomfortable.

- **Seeking help:** Many of us require support, whether from professionals, support groups, or loved ones. Willingness is the foundation for seeking and accepting help, as it acknowledges that recovery cannot be done in isolation.

- **Commitment to recovery:** Recovery is an ongoing journey that can be challenging. Willingness to stay committed to this process, even in the face of setbacks, is crucial for long-term success.

- **Personal growth:** Recovery often leads to profound personal growth and self-discovery. Willingness allows us to embrace this growth, to learn from our experiences, and to evolve into healthier, more resilient individuals.

- **Embracing accountability:** Being willing to take responsibility for past actions and their consequences is a key aspect of recovery. It involves making amends and making things right with those who may have been hurt.

- **Relinquishing control:** Willingness also involves acknowledging that control is often an illusion and that some aspects of recovery are beyond our control. This can involve letting go of the idea that we can manage everything on our own.

- **Positive mindset:** Willingness often leads to a more positive mindset. It encourages us to focus on the possibilities and opportunities that recovery offers rather than dwelling on the difficulties.

- **Resilience:** Recovery can be a challenging journey with its share of ups and downs. Willingness cultivates resilience, allowing us to persevere even when facing obstacles and setbacks.

What are ways to apply willingness?

- **Embrace a growth mindset:** Adopt a growth mindset by recognizing that change is possible and that personal growth is a continuous journey. Approach recovery with an attitude of curiosity, learning, and adaptability.

- **Acknowledge your challenges:** Recognize the challenges and obstacles you face in your recovery. Instead of avoiding or denying them, confront these challenges with a willingness to address them head-on.

- **Seek support and guidance:** Be open to seeking support from various sources, including therapists, support groups, sponsors, or trusted friends and family. Acknowledge that recovery often requires assistance and guidance from others.

- **Stay committed to change:** Maintain your commitment to change by regularly reviewing your recovery goals and affirming your willingness to work towards them. Keep these goals visible and remind yourself of your commitment.

- **Take responsibility:** Accept responsibility for your past actions and the consequences of your addiction. Willingness includes making amends, if appropriate, and working towards a better future.

- **Stay open-minded:** Be open to trying new approaches and strategies in your recovery. What may have worked for others might not work for you, so a willingness to experiment and adapt is valuable.

- **Learn from setbacks:** Understand that setbacks are a natural part of recovery. Instead of viewing them as failures, consider them as opportunities to learn and grow. Approach setbacks with resilience and a willingness to persevere.

- **Maintain a support network:** Build and maintain a strong support network of individuals who understand your journey. Willingness includes reaching out to these people when you need guidance or a listening ear.

- ✿ **Practice self-compassion:** Be kind and patient with yourself. Willingness involves accepting your imperfections and understanding that personal growth takes time. Treat yourself with the same compassion you would offer to a friend.

- ✿ **Daily reflection:** Spend time each day reflecting on your willingness to change. Write in a journal or engage in mindfulness practices to reinforce your commitment to recovery.

Willingness is an essential quality that empowers those of us in recovery to embrace change, seek help, commit to our journey, grow personally, and navigate the challenges of recovery with a positive and resilient mindset. It is a fundamental attribute that underpins many of the positive changes and progress made during the recovery process.

"Regardless of what you think or feel or wish to be true, true values are reflected in your choices and actions." — Mark Manson

INTEGRITY

What is the spiritual principle of integrity?

Integrity is about living in accordance with your values and principles. Integrity refers to the consistency between one's values, beliefs, and actions. It means committing to being honest with yourself and others and sticking to what you believe is right, even when it's tough. Integrity involves being reliable, taking responsibility for your actions, and being genuine. It's about having the courage to stay true to yourself and do what you believe is right, even if others disagree. Being humble, reflecting on your actions, being open to learning, and showing kindness to others are all part of maintaining spiritual integrity. Overall, it's seen as an important quality for a fulfilling and meaningful life in various spiritual and philosophical beliefs.

How does integrity help recovery?

- **Alignment with values and internal consistency:** Integrity involves living in accordance with your values and principles. In recovery, we often work to rediscover and embrace positive values. Acting with integrity means aligning behaviors with these values, fostering a sense of internal consistency.

- **Building self-trust:** Addiction often erodes self-trust as we engage in behaviors that conflict with our values. Developing integrity means rebuilding trust in ourselves by making choices that align with a healthier lifestyle.

- **Trust in relationships:** Integrity contributes to building and rebuilding trust in relationships. As those of us in recovery demonstrate consistent, honest behavior, it can positively impact our relationships with family, friends, and the recovery community.

- **Accountability:** Acknowledging mistakes and taking responsibility for our actions is a key aspect of integrity. In recovery, we learn to be accountable for the consequences of our choices, which is essential for personal growth.

- **Staying true when faced with challenges:** Recovery often involves building resilience by facing challenges, cravings, and triggers. Upholding our integrity can serve as a guiding principle during difficult times, helping us make choices that support our recovery goals rather than succumbing to old patterns.

- **Authenticity:** Embracing integrity involves being authentic and true to ourselves. In recovery, this means letting go of the false self, created by addiction, so we can discover and embrace the genuine self. This authenticity is empowering and contributes to a more stable recovery.

What are ways to cultivate integrity?

- **Self-reflection:** Take time for introspection to understand personal values and beliefs. Reflect on past actions and their alignment (or misalignment) with these values. Identify areas where there may be discrepancies between values and behavior.

- **Set clear personal values:** Clearly define personal values that align with a sense of integrity. Prioritize values that support recovery, such as honesty, responsibility, and accountability.

- **Goal setting:** Set realistic and achievable goals that align with personal values. Break down larger goals into smaller, manageable steps to make progress more tangible.

- ✤ **Develop a moral compass:** Establish a moral or ethical framework to guide decision-making. Consider seeking guidance from spiritual or philosophical beliefs to reinforce ethical principles.

- ✤ **Practice honesty:** Be honest with yourself about your thoughts, emotions, and actions. Practice open and honest communication with others, especially in relationships affected by addiction.

- ✤ **Accountability:** Take responsibility for past actions without blaming others. When mistakes are made, acknowledge them, learn from them, and make amends when possible.

- ✤ **Mindfulness and awareness:** Cultivate mindfulness to stay present in the moment. Pay attention to impulses, triggers, and potential conflicts between values and actions.

- ✤ **Surround yourself with support:** Build a support network of individuals who share similar values and support recovery. Seek guidance from mentors, counselors, or other forms of support.

- ✤ **Educate yourself:** Learn about ethical principles and moral values. Understanding the philosophical and psychological aspects of integrity can deepen your commitment to living with integrity.

Fostering integrity is an ongoing, dynamic process involving self-reflection, commitment, and consistent effort. It involves self-compassion, a commitment to personal growth, and a willingness to learn from experiences. Regular self-assessment and adjustments to behavior and goals contribute to the development of a more authentic and integrated life in recovery.

> *"The single most important piece of advice about prayer is one word: Begin!"* — Peter Kreeft

SPIRITUAL PRACTICES

PRAYER

What is the spiritual practice of prayer?

Prayer is a universal phenomenon embedded in various religious and spiritual traditions. It serves as a conduit for communication between us and a higher power, facilitating expressions of gratitude, devotion, and the seeking of guidance. Whether through praise, requests for assistance, or moments of contemplation, prayer plays a multifaceted role. It acts as a means of worship, allowing us to convey reverence and acknowledgment of the greatness attributed to our higher power. Additionally, prayer serves as a channel for seeking wisdom, guidance, and clarity during challenging circumstances. It embodies a meditative and contemplative aspect, offering a space for reflection and inner connection. The communal nature of prayer fosters unity and a shared spiritual experience among believers, emphasizing its role not only as an individual practice but also as a collective and ritualistic expression. Furthermore, prayer can encompass the acts of confessing sins, seeking forgiveness, and expressing gratitude for life's blessings. Overall, prayer is a dynamic and deeply ingrained spiritual practice that takes on diverse forms and meanings across different cultural and religious contexts.

How does prayer help recovery?

- **Spiritual connection:** Prayer often involves seeking a connection with a higher power or a spiritual force. This sense of connection can provide us with a feeling of support and guidance, offering a source of strength during challenging times in the recovery journey.

- **Coping mechanism:** Prayer can serve as a constructive coping mechanism. Engaging in prayer provides a moment of reflection and a focused, positive activity, offering an alternative to negative or harmful coping strategies that may have been part of the person's past.

- **Mindfulness and reflection:** Engaging in prayer often involves moments of mindfulness and self-reflection. This can be particularly beneficial for us, helping us stay present in the moment, reflecting on our thoughts and actions, and fostering a deeper understanding of ourselves.

- **Emotional regulation:** Prayer may contribute to emotional regulation by providing a space to express and process emotions. This can be especially helpful when dealing with the intense emotional challenges that often accompany the recovery process.

- **Community support:** Many recovery programs incorporate spiritual aspects, including communal prayers or shared spiritual activities. Participating in these practices fosters a sense of community, providing us with a supportive network and a shared sense of purpose.

- **Guidance and clarity:** Prayer can serve as a means of seeking guidance and clarity. This can be particularly relevant, helping us navigate challenging decisions, gain insight into our own values, and find a sense of direction.

- **Hope and positivity:** Engaging in prayer can instill a sense of hope and positivity. Believing in a higher power or seeking spiritual guidance can provide us with an optimistic outlook, which is essential for maintaining resilience and motivation during the recovery journey.

- **Acts of confession and forgiveness:** Prayer often involves acts of confession, seeking forgiveness, and expressing gratitude. This can be a powerful tool for us to address past mistakes, seek forgiveness from ourselves and others, and work towards emotional healing.

What are ways to practice prayer?

- ❦ **Establish a routine:** Set aside specific times each day for prayer. Consistency is key, and having a routine can help anchor your practice and make it a regular part of your day.

- ❦ **Morning gratitude prayer:** Start your day with a gratitude prayer. Express thanks for the positive aspects of your life, your sobriety, and the opportunities for growth ahead.

- ❦ **Evening reflection prayer:** Before bedtime, engage in a reflection prayer. Review your day, acknowledging both successes and challenges. Use this time to seek guidance and express gratitude for the strength to overcome obstacles.

- ❦ **Prayer for strength:** Create prayers specifically focused on gaining strength to resist urges and face difficult situations. Seek the inner strength necessary for maintaining sobriety.

- ❦ **Prayer for healing:** Offer prayers for emotional and spiritual healing. This can be a way to process past traumas and seek divine assistance in the healing process.

- ❦ **Prayer for guidance:** Seek guidance in your prayers, asking for clarity and wisdom in making positive decisions for your recovery. Trust that you are being led down the right path.

- ❦ **Prayer for patience:** Recovery is a journey that requires patience. Include prayers that ask for the patience to navigate challenges, understanding that progress may take time.

- ❦ **Community prayer:** Participate in group prayers or attend religious services where the community comes together to pray. This sense of shared spirituality can provide additional support and a sense of belonging.

- ✤ **Sacred text/scripture:** If you're inclined towards religious traditions, consider practicing a contemplative reading of text/scripture. This involves reading a passage, meditating on it, praying about it, and then contemplating its meaning in your life.

- ✤ **Mindful prayer:** Engage in mindful prayer by being fully present in the moment. Focus on the words you are saying, the feelings you are experiencing, and the connection with a higher power.

Prayer can be a valuable tool in the recovery process, providing us with a sense of spiritual connection, support, and guidance. The practice of prayer is personal, and we can each find different approaches that resonate with us. It's important to explore various methods and discover what feels most meaningful and effective for your own recovery journey.

"The you that goes in one side of the meditation experience is not the same you that comes out the other side." — Bhante Henepola Gunaratana

MEDITATION

What is the spiritual practice of meditation?

Meditation involves training your mind to concentrate and redirect thoughts, aiming to achieve mental clarity, relaxation, and heightened awareness. While its origins are rooted in various religious and spiritual traditions, meditation is also widely embraced for its secular benefits, such as stress reduction, improved concentration, and overall well-being. The practice takes diverse forms, but most techniques share common elements like focused attention, controlled breathing, and a tranquil environment.

Mindfulness meditation encourages present-moment awareness without judgment. Loving-kindness meditation fosters feelings of compassion. And transcendental meditation involves repeating a mantra for a state of relaxed awareness. Other variations include guided meditation, where we are led through visualizations, and Zen meditation (Zazen), which centers on breath observation without attachment to thoughts. Regular meditation is recommended to experience its numerous benefits, ranging from reduced stress to increased self-awareness and a sense of inner peace. We can choose the meditation style that resonates most with us for consistent practice. Whether approached as a secular practice for mental health or as a spiritual journey toward self-discovery, meditation remains a versatile and transformative tool.

How does meditation help recovery?

- **Stress reduction:** Meditation is known to be effective in reducing stress levels. In recovery, stress can be a significant trigger for relapse, so learning to manage stress through meditation can be crucial.

- **Emotional regulation:** Meditation helps us become more aware of our thoughts and emotions without being overwhelmed by them. This increased awareness can aid in emotional regulation, allowing us to respond to challenging situations in a more balanced and mindful way.

- **Increased self-awareness:** Meditation encourages self-reflection and self-awareness. This heightened awareness can help us recognize the underlying causes of our addictive behaviors and address them more effectively.

- **Mindfulness:** Mindfulness is a key component of many meditation practices. Being present in the moment without judgment can help us break free from automatic, habitual responses, allowing for more conscious decision-making.

- **Improved concentration:** Regular meditation practice is associated with improved concentration and focus. This can be particularly beneficial in recovery, as we often need to concentrate on our treatment plans, therapy sessions, and making positive lifestyle changes.

- **Coping with cravings:** Meditation provides us with tools to observe and manage cravings without automatically giving in to them. By cultivating mindfulness, we can develop the ability to sit with discomfort without seeking immediate relief through substance use.

- **Better sleep:** Many of us in recovery struggle with sleep disturbances. Meditation can promote relaxation and improve sleep quality, contributing to overall well-being.

- **Building resilience:** Meditation fosters resilience by helping us develop a more balanced and accepting perspective toward life's challenges. This resilience can be crucial in navigating the ups and downs of the recovery journey.

- **Connection with spirituality:** For some of us, meditation can be a way to connect with our spiritual beliefs or a higher power. This can provide a sense of purpose and support in the recovery process.

What are ways to practice meditation?

- **Mindfulness meditation:** Focus on your breath. Sit comfortably, close your eyes, and bring your attention to your breath. Notice the sensations of each inhale and exhale. If your mind wanders, gently bring it back to your breath.

- **Body scan:** Pay attention to each part of your body, starting from your toes and moving up to the top of your head. Notice any sensations without judgment.

- **Loving-kindness meditation:** Send positive wishes. Sit comfortably and focus on generating feelings of love and compassion. Send positive wishes to yourself, loved ones, acquaintances, and even those you may have conflicts with.

- **Guided meditation:** Use guided meditation recordings. There are numerous guided meditations available online or through meditation apps. These recordings often provide instructions and visualizations, making it easier for beginners to follow along.

- **Mantra meditation:** Choose a mantra. Select a word, phrase, or sound that holds personal significance or represents positive qualities. Repeat the mantra silently or aloud, focusing your attention on it.

- **Breath awareness meditation:** Focus on your breath variations. Pay attention to different aspects of your breath, such as its rhythm, depth, and the pauses between inhalation and exhalation. This helps anchor your awareness in the present moment.

- ✤ **Movement with meditative awareness:** Pay attention to the sensations in your body as you use movements such as in yoga or Tai Chi to coordinate your breath with your movements.

- ✤ **Nature meditation:** Spend time outdoors. Find a quiet natural setting, whether it's a park, garden, or trail. Sit or walk mindfully, paying attention to the sights, sounds, and sensations around you.

- ✤ **Visualization meditation:** Create mental images. Picture a peaceful scene or visualize positive outcomes for your recovery journey. Use the power of your imagination to evoke feelings of calm and optimism.

- ✤ **Gratitude meditation:** Reflect on what you're grateful for. Take a few moments to consider the positive aspects of your life. Focus on feelings of gratitude for the people, experiences, and opportunities that contribute to your well-being.

When starting a meditation practice in recovery, it's essential to approach it with an open mind and be patient with yourself. Consistency is key, and even short daily sessions can yield positive results over time. Additionally, consider exploring different techniques to find what resonates best with you. It can be helpful to seek guidance from experienced meditation instructors or use meditation apps that provide structured sessions and support.

"Mindfulness is the aware, balanced acceptance of the present experience. It isn't more complicated than that. It is opening to or receiving the present moment, pleasant or unpleasant, just as it is, without either clinging to it or rejecting it." - Sylvia Boorstein

MINDFULNESS

What is the spiritual practice of mindfulness?

Mindfulness is a spiritual and psychological practice that has its roots in Buddhist traditions but has been adapted for various secular and religious contexts. It involves cultivating a heightened awareness of the present moment, encouraging us to focus on our current experiences without judgment or attachment to past or future concerns. As we practice, we aim to observe thoughts and emotions as they arise, adopting a non-judgmental stance and accepting things as they are. Common elements include present moment awareness, non-judgmental observation of thoughts and feelings, mindful breathing, body scans, mindful movement, and the practice of acceptance and letting go. While rooted in Eastern spirituality, mindfulness has found broad application in secular settings, with various therapeutic approaches incorporating it to address stress, anxiety, and depression. Its universal nature allows those of us from diverse religious or non-religious backgrounds to engage in the practice, promoting mental and physical well-being.

How does mindfulness help recovery?

- **Increased self-awareness:** Mindfulness encourages us to be fully present in the moment, promoting heightened self-awareness. This awareness helps us recognize our thoughts, emotions, and triggers related to addictive behaviors, fostering a deeper understanding of the underlying issues contributing to our addiction.

- **Craving management:** Mindfulness techniques, such as mindful breathing or observing sensations without attachment, can be powerful tools in managing cravings. By staying present with the sensations and emotions without reacting impulsively, we are more likely to ride out the intensity of cravings and make more conscious choices.

- **Stress reduction:** Mindfulness is renowned for its stress-reducing effects. In recovery, stress is a common trigger for relapse. Mindfulness practices, such as meditation or mindful movement, provide us with practical tools to cope with stress, promoting emotional balance and resilience.

- **Acceptance and non-judgment:** Mindfulness encourages a non-judgmental attitude toward our thoughts and feelings. This acceptance can be transformative in recovery, helping us let go of guilt, shame, and self-criticism. It creates a space for self-compassion, which is crucial for building a positive and supportive self-image.

- **Improved emotional regulation:** Mindfulness practices train us to observe our emotions without being overwhelmed by them. This skill is valuable in recovery, as it empowers us to respond to challenging emotions in a measured and thoughtful way rather than resorting to impulsive and potentially harmful behaviors.

- **Enhanced focus and concentration:** Addiction often disrupts cognitive functions, including concentration. Mindfulness practices, which involve cultivating focused attention, can help improve concentration and cognitive clarity, supporting us in our daily tasks and decision-making.

- **Building resilience:** Mindfulness fosters a sense of inner strength and resilience. By developing a consistent mindfulness practice, those of us in recovery can build mental and emotional resilience, helping us navigate the inevitable ups and downs of life without turning to substances for escape.

- **Connection with the present:** Mindfulness emphasizes being in the present moment, steering us away from dwelling on past mistakes or worrying about the future. This focus on the present can be liberating and empowering, allowing us to approach each moment with intention and clarity.

What are ways to practice mindfulness?

- **Mindful breathing:** Find a quiet space to sit comfortably. Focus your attention on your breath. Inhale and exhale slowly, paying attention to the sensations of each breath. If your mind wanders, gently bring it back to the breath.

- **Body scan:** Lie down or sit comfortably. Bring your attention to different parts of your body, starting from your toes and moving up to your head. Notice any sensations, tension, or areas of discomfort without judgment.

- **Mindful meditation:** Set aside a few minutes for meditation. Choose a comfortable posture and focus on a specific point of attention (breath, a mantra, or a guided meditation). Allow thoughts to come and go without attachment, bringing your focus back to your chosen point.

- **Mindful walking:** Take a slow walk, paying attention to each step. Notice the sensations in your feet and legs as they move. Engage your senses by observing your surroundings, feeling the breeze, or listening to the sounds around you.

- **Mindful eating:** Pay full attention to each bite of your meal. Notice the flavors, textures, and smells. Chew slowly and savor the experience without rushing.

- **Awareness of thoughts**: Take moments throughout the day to observe your thoughts without judgment. Notice any patterns or triggers related to addiction. Acknowledge thoughts without reacting to them impulsively.

- **Mindful activities:** Engage in everyday activities with full attention, such as washing dishes, gardening, or cleaning. Pay attention to the sensory details and the physical sensations involved in the task.

- **Yoga and mindful movement**: Practice yoga or other mindful movement activities. Focus on the connection between breath and movement. These activities can help release tension and promote overall well-being.

- **Guided mindfulness Apps or resources:** Use mindfulness apps or online resources that provide guided meditations and exercises.

Consistency is key when incorporating mindfulness into your recovery. Start with short sessions and gradually increase the duration as you become more comfortable. It's essential to approach mindfulness with a gentle and non-judgmental attitude, allowing yourself the time and space to develop the practice at your own pace. Additionally, combining mindfulness practices with other aspects of a comprehensive recovery plan can provide us with a holistic set of tools for sustained recovery and improved overall well-being.

> *"You yourself, as much as anybody in the entire universe, deserve your love and affection."*
> — Buddha

SELF-LOVE

What is the spiritual practice of self-love?

Self-love involves deliberately engaging in actions and adopting attitudes aimed at fostering a positive and compassionate relationship with yourself. It encompasses a variety of practical approaches, such as maintaining positive self-talk and treating yourself with kindness and encouragement. Prioritizing self-care activities, setting and enforcing healthy boundaries, and practicing mindfulness through meditation will contribute to mental and emotional well-being. Expressing gratitude for positive aspects of life, forgiving yourself for past mistakes, and celebrating personal achievements are integral components of this practice. Surrounding yourself with positive influences, engaging in activities that bring joy, and reflecting on values and goals contribute to a more authentic and self-loving existence. Adopting a growth-oriented mindset, practicing self-compassion during challenging times, and using affirmations to reinforce positive self-images are essential elements. Creative self-expression, continuous learning, and seeking support when needed also contribute to the ongoing journey of self-love.

How does self-love help recovery?

- **Builds self-esteem:** Engaging in self-love activities helps us build a positive self-image and boost self-esteem. This is crucial in recovery, where we may have struggled with feelings of shame and guilt.

- **Fosters a sense of worthiness:** Self-love emphasizes that we are deserving of happiness, health, and fulfillment. This shift in mindset can counteract feelings of unworthiness that may be associated with addictive behaviors.

- **Reduces reliance on external validation:** Many of us often benefit from developing an internal focus of validation, where our sense of worth comes from within rather than relying solely on external sources. Self-love supports this internal validation process.

- **Boosts motivation:** Loving yourself can be a powerful motivator for positive change. When we genuinely care about our well-being, we are more likely to stay committed to our recovery journey and make choices that align with our long-term goals.

- **Promotes personal responsibility:** Taking responsibility for our own well-being is a fundamental aspect of self-love. This sense of agency can empower us to actively participate in our healing journey.

- **Encourages forgiveness:** Recovery often involves addressing past mistakes and regrets. Self-love promotes forgiveness, both of yourself and others, allowing us to let go of the burdens of the past and focus on a positive and hopeful future.

What are ways to practice self-love?

- **Positive affirmations:** Use positive affirmations to reinforce self-love and challenge negative self-talk. Affirmations can help shift your mindset and promote a more positive and loving relationship with yourself.

- **Set realistic goals:** Break down larger goals into smaller, more achievable tasks. Celebrate your accomplishments, no matter how small, to build a sense of achievement and self-worth.

- **Set boundaries:** Establishing healthy boundaries is a crucial aspect of self-love. Learn to say no to things that deplete your energy and yes to those that nourish your well-being.

- **Attend support groups:** Connect with others who are on a similar recovery journey. Support groups offer a sense of community, understanding, and encouragement.

- **Express gratitude:** Regularly express gratitude for the positive aspects of your life. Focus on what you appreciate about yourself and your experiences.

- **Seek professional support:** Consider therapy or counseling to address underlying issues and work through challenges. A mental health professional can provide guidance and support tailored to your individual needs.

- **Forgive yourself:** Practice self-compassion and forgiveness. Understand that everyone makes mistakes and that recovery is a journey. Letting go of guilt and shame is essential for building self-love.

- **Surround yourself with positive influences:** Build a supportive network of friends and family who uplift and encourage you. Distance yourself from negative influences that may hinder your progress.

- **Celebrate milestones:** Acknowledge and celebrate your achievements in recovery, whether it's a day, a week, a month, or more. Recognizing your progress reinforces a positive self-view.

Self-love involves self-reflection, self-compassion, and a commitment to nurturing your well-being emotionally. Practicing self-love is an ongoing process, and it's important to be patient and compassionate with yourself. Each person's journey is unique, so explore different strategies and find what works best for you in fostering a loving and supportive relationship with yourself.

"To contemplate is to look at shadows."
— Victor Hugo

CONTEMPLATION

What is the spiritual practice of contemplation?

Contemplation, especially in spiritual contexts, involves a profound engagement with deep thought, reflection, and meditation. It surpasses mere intellectual analysis, aiming to establish connections with deeper levels of understanding, insight, and awareness. Rooted in various religious and philosophical traditions, contemplation encompasses diverse methods and objectives. Contemplation typically unfolds in an atmosphere of silence and stillness, achieved through meditation or withdrawal from external distractions.

At its core, contemplation emphasizes inner reflection, prompting us to explore our thoughts, emotions, and experiences to cultivate increased self-awareness. In spiritual settings, contemplation often includes the pursuit of connection with a higher power, higher consciousness, or our elevated self through prayer, meditation on sacred texts, or other rituals. It also involves delving into profound existential questions about existence, life's purpose, and the interconnectedness of all things, facilitating a deeper understanding of our place in the world. Additionally, certain contemplative practices aim to transcend the ego, encouraging us to release attachments, overcome desires, and experience a sense of unity with the larger world. Virtue cultivation, particularly virtues such as compassion, love, humility, and patience, represents another aspect of contemplation, with practitioners striving to comprehend and embody these virtues in their daily lives.

How does contemplation help recovery?

- **Increased self-awareness:** Contemplation encourages us to reflect on our thoughts, emotions, and behaviors. This self-awareness is crucial in recovery as it helps us recognize triggers, patterns, and the root causes of our challenges.

- **Emotional regulation:** Contemplation provides an opportunity to explore and understand emotions without judgment. This can be particularly helpful in developing healthier coping mechanisms and emotional regulation skills. Recognizing and processing emotions can be a key component of recovery.

- **Clarifying values and goals:** Contemplation allows us to explore our values and set meaningful goals for ourselves. This process can help align our actions with our values, providing a sense of purpose and direction in the recovery journey.

- **Building resilience:** Contemplation fosters resilience by encouraging us to approach challenges with a thoughtful and measured mindset. Developing resilience is essential to overcoming setbacks and maintaining long-term recovery.

- **Improved decision-making:** Contemplation allows us to think more deeply about our choices and actions. This increased reflection can lead to more thoughtful and intentional decision-making, reducing the likelihood of impulsive or harmful behaviors.

- **Connection to spirituality:** For some of us, contemplation involves a spiritual or existential dimension. Exploring our spirituality can provide a sense of purpose, connection, and support, which can be especially meaningful in the recovery process.

- **Cognitive restructuring:** Contemplation allows us to challenge and reframe negative thought patterns. This cognitive restructuring can be instrumental in changing harmful beliefs and behaviors associated with addiction.

- **Promoting personal growth:** Contemplation can be a tool for personal growth and development. It encourages us to learn from our experiences, make positive changes, and evolve as individuals, fostering a sense of ongoing improvement.

- **Community and support:** Contemplation is not always a solitary activity. Group contemplative practices or discussions can foster a sense of community and support, providing those of us in recovery with a network of like-minded individuals who share similar goals.

What are ways to practice contemplation?

- **Daily reflection:** Create a habit of reflecting on your day, acknowledging both challenges and accomplishments. Consider how you can learn and grow from each experience.

- **Guided meditation:** Use guided meditation sessions to explore your thoughts and emotions. There are many resources available, including apps and online platforms.

- **Silent retreats:** Attend silent retreats to create space for deep contemplation and self-inquiry. Disconnect from external stimuli and immerse yourself in quiet reflection.

- **Journaling:** Maintain a recovery journal to document thoughts, emotions, and experiences. Reflecting on daily events and challenges can offer insights into patterns and triggers.

- **Visualization exercises:** Engage in guided visualization exercises, picturing positive outcomes and envisioning your path to recovery.

- **Nature contemplation:** Spend time outdoors, immersing yourself in nature. Reflect on the beauty around you and the sense of calm it provides.

- ❧ **Deep reading:** Read literature that encourages self-reflection and personal growth. Take the time to contemplate the messages and insights.

- ❧ **Community sharing:** Engage in group discussions or support meetings where individuals share their experiences and insights. Learn from others and offer your perspectives.

It's important to explore various contemplative practices and discover what resonates with you personally. Consistency is key, so integrating these practices into your daily or weekly routine can contribute to ongoing self-reflection and growth in recovery. Seeking guidance from therapists, support groups, or spiritual mentors can enhance the effectiveness of your contemplative practices.

"We not only nurture our sacred relationships through ritual, but we are nurtured by them as well. In ritual, we move, and we are moved."
— Alison Leigh Lilly

SACRED RITUALS

What is the spiritual practice of sacred rituals?

Sacred rituals encompass specific actions or ceremonies filled with symbolic meaning within a particular religious or spiritual context. These intentional and purposeful actions extend beyond their physical aspects, aiming to establish and strengthen a connection with our spiritual nature or a higher power. The primary objective of sacred rituals is to foster a sense of communion, allowing us to express devotion and enhance our spiritual connection. Participation in these rituals allows us to express deep commitment to our faith through acts of worship, gratitude, and reverence.

While the specifics of rituals vary across diverse religions and spiritual traditions, they share common elements such as the use of symbols, repetition of words or actions, and an overall atmosphere of respect and reverence. The rituals are meticulously designed to create a sacred or holy environment. Whether through prayer, meditation, or other ceremonial practices, we can engage in these rituals to experience a heightened sense of the sacred in our spiritual journey.

Sacred rituals also provide a structured framework for expressing faith, aiding us in navigating our spiritual beliefs and fostering a sense of continuity and tradition. The structure inherent in these rituals becomes a guide, helping us to connect with a higher power and live out our faith in meaningful ways.

How do sacred rituals help recovery?

- **Structure and routine**: Sacred rituals provide a structured and regular routine, helping us to establish stability and predictability in our daily lives.

- **Mindfulness:** Many sacred rituals emphasize being present in the moment, promoting mindfulness. This can be particularly beneficial for recovery, encouraging us to focus on the present and manage stressors effectively.

- **Emotional expression:** Sacred rituals often include elements of emotional expression, allowing us to express and process our emotions in a healthy and constructive manner.

- **Transcendence and transformation:** Sacred rituals often offer a transcendent experience, allowing us to connect with something greater than ourselves. This can foster a sense of purpose, meaning, and personal transformation in recovery.

- **Spiritual exploration:** Sacred rituals provide a platform for spiritual exploration and self-discovery, allowing us to deepen our understanding of our own beliefs and values.

- **Coping mechanism:** Sacred rituals serve as a positive coping mechanism, offering an alternative to unhealthy behaviors or substance use during times of stress or challenge.

- **Reflection and contemplation:** Sacred rituals often include moments of reflection and contemplation, providing us with an opportunity to assess our progress in recovery and set intentions for the future.

- **Holistic well-being:** Sacred rituals often address our holistic well-being while considering our physical, emotional, and spiritual needs in the recovery process.

- **Personalized support:** We can personalize sacred rituals to align with our unique beliefs and preferences, making them a customized and meaningful aspect of our recovery journey.

- **Creating a safe and sacred space:** Sacred rituals often involve specific environments or settings that are considered sacred. Creating a safe and sacred space can offer us a sense of sanctuary and tranquility, supporting our overall well-being.

What are ways to practice sacred rituals?

- **Morning gratitude practice:** Start the day by expressing gratitude for positive aspects of life, fostering a positive mindset.

- **Prayer of surrender:** Start or end the day with a prayer of surrender, acknowledging the need for support and guidance in the recovery journey.

- **Affirmation ritual:** Create a list of empowering affirmations and recite them daily, reinforcing a positive self-image and commitment to recovery.

- **Morning meditation:** Begin each day with a focused meditation session to center the mind and set positive intentions for the day.

- **Candle lighting ceremony:** Light a candle with a specific intention for healing and transformation.

- **Prayer rituals:** Engage in prayer as a way to connect with a higher power and seek guidance.

- **Daily spiritual reading:** To inspire and uplift yourself, read spiritual texts or literature that align with your beliefs.

- **Digital detox ritual:** Dedicate specific times to disconnect from electronic devices for inner reflection and peace.

- ꙮ **Release and let go ceremony:** Write down negative thoughts or emotions on paper, then burn or bury them as a symbolic act of release.

- ꙮ **Evening reflection:** Reflect on the events of the day, acknowledging achievements and areas for improvement.

These rituals can provide structure, support, and spiritual growth. It's important to note that the effectiveness of sacred rituals in supporting recovery can vary from person to person. The choice of rituals should be personalized to reflect your beliefs, values, and cultural background and contribute positively to your recovery and well-being. Additionally, you may find it beneficial to integrate these rituals as part of a comprehensive recovery approach that includes spiritual mentorship, professional counseling, and support groups.

> *"With every act of self-care your authentic self gets stronger, and the critical, fearful mind gets weaker. Every act of self-care is a powerful declaration: I am on my side, I am on my side, each day I am more and more on my own side."* — Susan Weiss Berry

SELF-CARE

What is the spiritual practice of self-care?

Self-care is a conscious and thoughtful approach to enhancing our overall well-being. It encompasses a diverse range of activities that address various dimensions of health, including the physical, mental, emotional, social, spiritual, and intellectual aspects. Physical self-care involves activities like regular exercise, sufficient sleep, maintaining a balanced diet, and ensuring proper hydration. Mental and emotional well-being is nurtured through practices such as mindfulness, meditation, journaling, and the establishment of healthy boundaries in relationships. Social self-care emphasizes positive interactions with friends and family, while spiritual self-care may include participation in spiritual practices or connecting with nature. Intellectual self-care involves continuous learning and the pursuit of personal interests. Adequate rest, relaxation, and engagement in leisure activities are vital components. Setting boundaries, practicing self-compassion, and expressing gratitude contribute to a comprehensive and individualized self-care routine. Ultimately, self-care allows us to customize our well-being practices according to our unique needs and preferences, promoting optimal health and fulfillment.

How does self-care help recovery?

- **Stress management:** Self-care practices, like deep breathing or meditation, help manage stress, a common trigger for relapse.

- **Mental well-being:** Practices such as therapy, mindfulness, and adequate sleep contribute to improved mental health, reducing the risk of mental health issues during recovery.

- **Physical health:** Regular exercise, proper nutrition, and sufficient sleep support overall physical health, positively impacting the recovery journey.

- **Enhanced self-esteem:** Engaging in self-care fosters a positive self-image and self-worth. This is particularly important in recovery, where we may be rebuilding our lives and working towards a healthier self-concept.

- **Burnout prevention:** Self-care practices prevent burnout by encouraging us to set realistic goals and take breaks, sustaining energy levels during recovery.

- **Building healthy habits:** Engaging in self-care routines helps establish healthy habits, replacing previous patterns associated with addiction.

- **Social support:** Social self-care involves maintaining positive relationships, which is crucial for a strong support system during recovery.

- **Routine and structure:** Establishing self-care routines contributes to a sense of structure and stability, essential elements in the recovery process.

- **Personal empowerment:** Engaging in self-care activities empowers us to take control of our well-being, fostering a proactive mindset.

What are ways to practice self-care?

- **Self-reflection:** Take time for self-reflection to understand your thoughts, feelings, and triggers. Journaling can be a helpful tool for this purpose.

- **Nature walks:** Spend time in nature, whether it's a short walk in a park or a hike in the mountains. Nature has a calming effect on the mind.

- **Intellectual stimulation:** Engage in activities that challenge your mind, such as reading, solving puzzles, or learning a new skill.

- **Digital detox:** Take breaks from electronic devices and social media. Disconnecting from screens can help reduce stress and improve your mental well-being.

- **Hot baths or showers:** Treat yourself to a warm bath or shower. This can be a simple and effective way to relax your muscles and clear your mind.

- **Yoga or stretching:** Incorporate gentle yoga or stretching exercises into your routine to improve flexibility, release tension, and promote relaxation.

- **Art therapy**: Engage in art therapy activities, such as drawing, painting, or sculpting, to express emotions and promote self-discovery.

- **Therapeutic writing:** Journal your thoughts and feelings to gain insight into your emotions and promote emotional release.

- **Regular exercise routine:** Establish a consistent exercise routine to boost your physical health and release endorphins.

- **Laughter therapy:** Engage in activities that make you laugh, whether it's watching a comedy show, spending time with humorous friends, or enjoying funny content.

- **Balanced nutrition:** Maintain a well-balanced diet to nourish your body and support overall physical well-being.

- ꞵ **Adequate sleep:** Prioritize and ensure you get enough restorative sleep each night for physical and mental recovery.

- ꞵ **Meditation and prayer:** Engage in meditation or prayer practices to connect with your spiritual beliefs and find inner peace.

- ꞵ **Self-compassion:** Be kind and compassionate to yourself. Acknowledge your progress and embrace self-love.

- ꞵ **Social connections:** Foster meaningful connections with friends, family, or a support network to strengthen your overall support system.

Self-care serves as a multifaceted tool that supports us by addressing our physical, emotional, and social needs. It fosters resilience, provides healthy coping mechanisms, and contributes to an overall positive and balanced lifestyle during the recovery journey. Self-care is a personalized journey, and it's essential to listen to your own needs and adjust these practices to fit your unique circumstances. If needed, consult with a healthcare professional or spiritual advisor for additional guidance.

"I write entirely to find out what I'm thinking, what I'm looking at, what I see, and what it means. What I want and what I fear." — Joan Didion

JOURNALING

What is the spiritual practice of journaling?

Journaling is a deeply personal and reflective endeavor that involves the regular recording of our thoughts, emotions, and experiences. It goes beyond the conventional act of documenting daily events; it serves as a tool for self-discovery, introspection, and connection with the inner self. In the realm of spirituality, journaling creates a sacred space where we can safely explore our beliefs, values, and the meaning we derive from life. Many of us find solace in expressing gratitude, prayers, or intentions within the pages of our journals, fostering a sense of connection to a higher power. Through this practice, we often uncover patterns in our thoughts and behaviors, gaining insights into our spiritual journey and personal growth. Journaling can also serve as a medium for processing challenges, seeking guidance, and documenting moments of inspiration or revelation. Ultimately, the spiritual practice of journaling is a contemplative and transformative process that deepens our connection with ourselves and the broader spiritual dimensions of life.

How does journaling help recovery?

- **Self-reflection:** Journaling provides a safe space for us to reflect on our thoughts, actions, and emotions, promoting self-awareness and understanding.

- **Emotional regulation:** Writing about feelings and experiences allows us to process and manage our emotions, promoting emotional well-being during the recovery journey.

- **Connecting with a higher power:** Journaling can be a means of communication with a higher power, allowing us to express prayers, seek guidance, and deepen our spiritual connection.

- **Personal growth:** Journaling serves as a documented journey of personal growth and transformation, providing inspiration and a reminder of progress made.

- **Accountability:** Keeping a journal creates a record of progress, setbacks, and achievements, fostering a sense of accountability and responsibility for our actions.

- **Celebrate successes:** Recording even small victories and milestones in a journal helps us acknowledge our achievements, reinforcing a positive mindset during the recovery process.

- **Stress reduction:** Expressing stressors and challenges in writing can be therapeutic, serving as a healthy outlet for releasing tension and reducing the likelihood of turning to unhealthy coping mechanisms.

- **Processing trauma:** For those of us dealing with trauma, journaling can be a therapeutic tool for exploring and processing painful experiences, facilitating healing in a structured and private manner.

- **Spiritual exploration:** Journaling encourages us to explore and document our spiritual beliefs, experiences, and insights, contributing to a deeper understanding of our spiritual path.

What are ways to journal?

- **Daily reflection journal:** Write about your day, experiences, thoughts, and emotions. Reflect on events, challenges, and personal insights. This form of journaling helps you process daily occurrences.

- **Stream of consciousness journaling:** Write without a specific plan or structure. Let your thoughts flow freely onto the paper. This can be a therapeutic way to explore your mind and uncover subconscious thoughts.

- **Visual journaling:** Express yourself through art. Use drawings, doodles, paintings, or collages to capture your thoughts and emotions visually. This creative form of journaling provides an alternative to traditional written expression.

- **Prayer journaling:** Write down your prayers and conversations with a higher power. Reflect on your spiritual journey, express gratitude, and seek guidance through your written words.

- **Sacred readings reflections:** Journal about words or specific passages that resonate with you. Explore the meanings and applications of these teachings in your life. Pose spiritual questions or dilemmas in your journal and explore possible answers. This can help you gain clarity and a deeper understanding of your beliefs.

- **Symbolic imagery:** Incorporate symbolic drawings or imagery that hold spiritual significance for you. Use your journal as a visual representation of your spiritual journey.

- **Ritual observations:** Document your experiences with spiritual rituals, ceremonies, or events. Reflect on the symbolism and significance of these practices in your spiritual life.

- **Prompt-based journaling:** Use prompts or questions to guide your writing. This approach can provide structure and inspiration, especially when you're not sure what to write about.

The most effective journaling style is the one that feels comfortable and meaningful to you. Experiment with these different journaling styles or combine elements to create a practice that suits your preferences and serves your personal growth and well-being. The keys to effective journaling in recovery are consistency and honesty.

Your journal is a private space for self-reflection, growth, and support on your journey to sustained recovery.

"The best way to not feel hopeless is to get up and do something. Don't wait for good things to happen to you. If you go out and make some good things happen, you will fill the world with hope, you will fill yourself with hope." — Barack Obama

SERVICE

What is the spiritual practice of service?

Service is a deeply rooted concept found across various spiritual traditions. At its core, this practice involves engaging in acts of kindness and support for others without expecting anything in return. Central to the philosophy of service is the idea of transcending one's ego and fostering a sense of compassion and interconnectedness with all beings. Practitioners undertake acts of service with selflessness, demonstrating a genuine concern for the well-being of others. Compassion is a guiding principle, urging us to understand and empathize with the suffering of others and motivating us to take action to alleviate that suffering. The practice is founded on the recognition of the interconnected nature of all life, emphasizing unity and harmony.

Mindfulness plays a crucial role, encouraging us to engage in service with full presence and intention rather than through mechanical or routine actions. Equality and respect for all individuals, regardless of their background or beliefs, are integral components of the spiritual practice of service. Practitioners cultivate gratitude for the opportunity to contribute positively to the lives of others, fostering humility and acknowledging the sacredness of service in the journey toward spiritual growth and interconnected well-being.

How does service help recovery?

- **Shifts focus away from self:** Engaging in acts of service redirects our attention away from our own challenges and struggles. By actively helping others, we can break the cycle of self-centered thinking and gain a broader perspective on life.

- **Fosters a sense of purpose:** Serving others provides a meaningful purpose beyond our personal struggles. Having a sense of purpose can be crucial for those of us in recovery, offering us a reason to get up in the morning and a source of motivation to stay on a positive path.

- **Builds a supportive community:** Many spiritual practices of service involve working within a community or group setting. This creates a supportive network of like-minded individuals who share common values and goals. Building connections with others who are also focused on service can provide a sense of belonging and encouragement during our recovery journey.

- **Develops empathy and compassion:** Service encourages us to connect with the needs and experiences of others. This cultivation of empathy and compassion can be transformative in the recovery process, helping us develop a deeper understanding of ourselves and others.

- **Provides a positive outlet:** Service acts as a positive and constructive outlet. Instead of turning to negative coping mechanisms, engaging in acts of service allows us to channel our energy into activities that contribute positively to the well-being of others.

- **Enhances self-esteem:** Accomplishing meaningful acts of service can boost self-esteem and self-worth. As we witness the positive impact we can have on others, it reinforces a positive self-image and contributes to a more optimistic outlook on life.

- **Offers a source of gratitude:** Engaging in service often involves recognizing and appreciating the blessings in our own lives. Practicing gratitude is a powerful tool in recovery, helping us focus on the positive aspects of our journey and reinforcing a mindset of appreciation.

- **Promotes spiritual growth:** Many spiritual traditions emphasize the connection between service and spiritual growth. Engaging in selfless acts aligns with the values of compassion, love, and interconnectedness, providing us with a spiritual foundation that can support our overall well-being.

What are ways to practice service?

- **Volunteer at a local charity:** Offer your time and skills to a local charity or nonprofit organization that aligns with your values.

- **Participate in community clean-up events:** Join efforts to clean and beautify public spaces in your community.

- **Mentor others in recovery:** Share your experiences and provide support to individuals who are earlier in their recovery journey.

- **Offer transportation assistance:** Help individuals in your community who may face transportation challenges, such as driving them to appointments or grocery shopping.

- **Become a listener:** Be there for others by offering a listening ear and emotional support when needed.

- **Share your skills:** Offer to teach a class or workshop based on your skills or hobbies, providing others with an opportunity to learn something new.

- **Serve at a homeless shelter:** Volunteer your time at a local homeless shelter, assisting with meals, clothing distribution, or other essential services.

- ✤ **Write inspirational notes:** Send handwritten notes of encouragement to individuals in recovery or those going through difficult times.

- ✤ **Hospital or nursing home visits:** Spend time with individuals in hospitals or nursing homes who may be in need of companionship and support.

- ✤ **Animal shelter assistance:** Volunteer at an animal shelter, providing care and attention to animals awaiting adoption.

Service can be a transformative and healing component of the recovery process. Service activities not only contribute positively to the well-being of others but also provide us with opportunities to build a support network and continue our personal growth journey, offering us a path to personal growth, community support, and a sense of purpose beyond our own struggles. The key is to find a form of service that resonates with your interests and strengths. Contributing positively to the lives of others can be a powerful and fulfilling aspect of the recovery journey.

> *"Spiritual community gives a sense of meaning and direction, and of life that's bigger than one's own. It's healing without therapy."* — Rabbi Omer-Man

COMMUNITY

What is the spiritual practice of community?

Community involves the deliberate gathering of individuals to foster a profound sense of connection, mutual support, and shared purpose. Across diverse spiritual traditions, community is regarded as a fundamental element in the journey of spiritual growth and overall well-being. Within these communities, there exists a recognition of the interconnectedness of all individuals, emphasizing that our personal well-being is intricately linked with the well-being of others. Members of spiritual communities provide each other with essential emotional support, wisdom-sharing, and assistance during challenging times. Formed around shared values and beliefs, these communities celebrate diversity while collectively embracing a set of common principles. Rituals, ceremonies, and shared practices reinforce a sense of belonging and shared purpose, contributing to the spiritual and personal growth of community members. Learning and growth opportunities, service to others, and conflict resolution are integral aspects of this practice. Guided by spiritual leaders who prioritize humility and service, spiritual communities aim to create an inclusive environment that fosters a deep sense of belonging and acceptance. In essence, the spiritual practice of community is about creating a supportive space where individuals can connect on a profound level, nurturing a shared journey of spiritual exploration.

How does community help recovery?

- **Sense of belonging:** Being part of a spiritual community fosters a sense of belonging, reducing feelings of isolation and loneliness that can be common during the recovery journey. This sense of connection can contribute to emotional stability and well-being.

- **Support system:** Spiritual communities often function as a built-in support system. Members share common goals and values, providing a network of people who can offer encouragement, empathy, and practical assistance.

- **Shared spiritual practices:** Engaging in spiritual practices within a community setting can provide a structured and consistent framework for personal growth. Regular rituals, prayers, or meditations can help us develop a sense of routine and purpose.

- **Learning and growth:** Many spiritual communities offer educational opportunities and discussions on topics related to personal development and spiritual growth. This continuous learning process can empower us to understand our selves better.

- **Opportunities for service:** Many spiritual communities emphasize service to others. Engaging in acts of service provides us with an opportunity to give back to the community, fostering a sense of purpose and contributing to a positive self-image.

- **Safe space for expression:** Spiritual communities often provide a safe and non-judgmental space for us to express our thoughts, feelings, and struggles. This open communication fosters a sense of acceptance and understanding.

- **Spiritual leadership:** Guidance from spiritual leaders within the community can offer inspiration and direction. These leaders often model principles such as humility, compassion, and service, which can be valuable for those of us navigating the challenges of recovery.

- **Crisis support:** In times of crisis or relapse, the community can offer immediate support. Having a group of people who are willing to help can prevent isolation and help us get back on track.

- **Development of healthy relationships:** Participating in a spiritual community encourages the formation of healthy relationships based on shared values. These connections can replace negative influences from the past and contribute to a more stable and positive social environment.

What are ways to practice community?

- **Attend support groups:** Regularly participate in recovery-oriented support groups such as Alcoholics Anonymous (AA) or Narcotics Anonymous (NA). These groups provide a safe space to share experiences, gain insights, and build a supportive network.

- **Join a sober living community:** Consider residing in a sober living community, where individuals in recovery live together in a supportive environment, reinforcing the commitment to a sober lifestyle.

- **Volunteer in the recovery community:** Offer your time and skills to organizations or initiatives focused on addiction recovery. This could involve assisting in support group meetings, organizing events, or providing mentorship to others in recovery.

- **Participate in church or spiritual gatherings:** Engage with a spiritual or religious community that aligns with your beliefs. Attend services, join study groups, or participate in community events to connect with like-minded individuals.

- **Create a recovery accountability group:** Form a small group of individuals in recovery who commit to supporting each other's goals. Regularly check in, share progress, and offer encouragement to maintain accountability.

- **Attend workshops and seminars:** Participate in workshops or seminars related to recovery, spirituality, or personal development. These events provide opportunities to connect with others who share similar interests and goals.

- **Connect online:** Utilize online platforms and forums dedicated to recovery and/or spirituality. Engage in discussions, share experiences, and offer support to others in virtual communities focused on sobriety.

- **Join fitness or wellness groups:** Participate in fitness classes, yoga, or wellness groups where individuals prioritize their physical and mental well-being. These environments often promote healthy lifestyles and positive connections.

- **Participate in alumni programs:** If you attended a treatment or rehabilitation program, explore alumni programs that facilitate ongoing connections with individuals who have completed the program.

- **Attend sober events:** Look for events in your community that cater to those in recovery, such as sober concerts, art exhibits, or recreational activities. These events provide opportunities to connect with like-minded individuals in a substance-free environment.

Community serves as a vital component in the recovery process by providing a supportive, understanding, and growth-oriented environment. It offers a network of people who share a common journey, fostering a sense of connection, accountability, and purpose on the path to recovery.

"Place your hands into soil to feel grounded. Wade in water to feel emotionally healed. Fill your lungs with fresh air to feel mentally clear. Raise your face to the heat of the sun and connect with that fire to feel your own immense power." — Victoria Erickson

NATURE

What is the spiritual practice of nature?

Nature encompasses a diverse range of beliefs and rituals that highlight a profound connection to the natural world. This spiritual approach involves cultivating a deep appreciation for nature and seeking transcendent experiences through interactions with the environment. Some adherents engage in nature worship, conducting rituals to honor elements like the sun, moon, trees, water, and animals. Eco-spirituality combines ecological awareness with spiritual values, emphasizing the interconnectedness of all living things and promoting environmental stewardship. Others practice meditation in natural settings to achieve inner peace and a sense of connection.

Nature-based rituals, such as seasonal celebrations, play a role in this spiritual practice, along with the animistic perspective that attributes spiritual essence or consciousness to animals, plants, inanimate objects, and natural phenomena. Additionally, shamanic practices within certain traditions involve rituals and ceremonies in natural settings to connect with spiritual forces or receive guidance from the natural world. It's important to recognize that the spiritual practice of nature is diverse, varying among individuals and cultures, with practitioners drawing inspiration from different traditions or developing personalized approaches rooted in a deep reverence for the natural world.

How does nature help recovery?

- **Mindfulness and stress reduction:** Nature provides a serene and calming environment, making it an ideal setting for mindfulness practices. Engaging in activities like walking, meditation, or simply being present in nature can help us manage stress, reduce anxiety, and promote overall mental well-being.

- **Connection and community:** The spiritual practice of being in touch with nature often emphasizes interconnectedness. Fostering a sense of connection to the natural world can extend to building supportive relationships with others. This sense of community can be crucial in the recovery process, providing understanding, encouragement, and a shared connection to a larger whole.

- **Physical exercise:** Many nature-based activities involve physical movement, such as hiking, jogging, or yoga in outdoor settings. Regular physical exercise is known to have positive effects on mood, energy levels, and overall health, contributing to the recovery journey.

- **Symbolic renewal:** Nature is often associated with cycles of renewal and growth. Engaging in the spiritual practice of spending time in nature allows us to symbolically connect with these natural processes, offering a metaphorical representation of personal transformation and renewal during the recovery journey.

- **Mind-body connection:** The holistic quality of the spiritual practice of engaging with nature encourages us to connect with both our physical and mental well-being. This integrated approach can enhance self-awareness, aiding in the recognition of triggers and stressors that may impact recovery.

- **Emotional healing:** Nature has the power to evoke a range of emotions, from awe and wonder to tranquility and joy.

Engaging in nature-based activities provides a space for emotional expression and healing, allowing us to explore and process our feelings in a supportive environment.

- **Sense of purpose:** The spiritual practice of connecting with nature often instills a sense of purpose and responsibility towards the Earth. This connection to a larger purpose can be transformative, helping us find meaning and motivation as we navigate the challenges of recovery.

What are ways to connect with nature?

- **Forest bathing (Shinrin-yoku):** Immerse yourself in the forest, focusing on the sights, sounds, and scents around you. This Japanese practice, known as shinrin-yoku, promotes a deep connection with nature for relaxation and well-being.

- **Sacred plant medicine:** Explore the spiritual and healing properties of plants. Engage in rituals involving herbs, flowers, or other natural elements, acknowledging their symbolic and medicinal significance.

- **Nature altars:** Create a nature altar in a special outdoor spot. Arrange stones, leaves, flowers, or other elements that resonate with you spiritually. Use the altar for reflection, meditation, or as a focal point for rituals.

- **Earth prayers and chants:** Practice earth-centric prayers or chants. Create or learn rituals that involve vocal expressions of gratitude, respect, or intentions for the well-being of the Earth.

- **Nature retreats:** Plan retreats or getaways in natural settings. Disconnect from technology and immerse yourself in the healing energies of nature to foster spiritual growth.

- **Nature-based ceremonies:** Design and participate in ceremonies that celebrate nature's cycles. This could include ceremonies for solstices, equinoxes, or other natural events that hold significance for you.

- ⚘ **Earth-based spirituality workshops:** Attend workshops or classes on earth-based spirituality. Learn about different traditions, rituals, and practices that integrate spiritual beliefs with a reverence for the Earth.

- ⚘ **Sacred site visits:** Explore natural sites that are considered sacred in various spiritual traditions. These could include mountains, lakes, or ancient groves. Take time for contemplation and reverence in these special places.

- ⚘ **Volunteer for environmental projects:** Contribute to the well-being of the environment by participating in local conservation or environmental projects. Working hands-on in nature fosters a sense of stewardship and connection to the Earth.

The spiritual practice of connecting with nature can vary widely among people and cultures, and there isn't a single, universally defined approach. We may draw inspiration from different spiritual or religious traditions or develop our own personalized practices based on a deep reverence for the natural world.

"You will not see anyone who is truly striving after his spiritual advancement who is not given to spiritual reading." — Athanasius of Alexandria

SACRED READING

What is the spiritual practice of sacred reading?

Sacred reading, devoid of specific religious affiliations, is a contemplative and interfaith approach to engaging with sacred texts. This transcultural practice attracts those of us seeking a profound connection with a higher power, universal truths, or deep wisdom present in various spiritual traditions. The central focus lies in a deliberate and meditative reading of chosen texts, such as scriptures, poetry, or philosophical writings. Rather than a hurried or analytical approach, practitioners emphasize a slow and reflective reading, delving beyond the literal meanings to explore layers of symbolism and metaphor. This contemplative process involves reflection, meditation, and moments of inner silence, encouraging us to connect with a deeper, intuitive understanding. The ultimate aim often revolves around personal transformation, where insights gained from sacred reading influence our values, actions, and spiritual journey. This inclusive practice allows those of us from diverse backgrounds to explore universal themes of wisdom and compassion, fostering a shared human endeavor to understand the mysteries of existence beyond specific religious dogmas.

How does sacred reading help recovery?

- **Reflection and self-discovery:** Sacred reading provides a structured and contemplative space for us to reflect on our experiences, fostering self-discovery and insight into the root causes of challenges in recovery.

- **Mindfulness and presence:** Engaging in sacred reading encourages mindfulness, helping us to stay grounded and focused on the present moment rather than dwelling on past mistakes or anxieties about the future.

- **Spiritual support:** Sacred texts offer spiritual or moral guidance, providing comfort, hope, and a sense of purpose that can be particularly beneficial for those of us navigating the challenges of recovery.

- **Values clarification:** The practice helps us clarify our values and find deeper meaning in life, offering a powerful motivator for sustaining recovery and making positive life choices aligned with our newfound understanding.

- **Community and connection:** Engaging in group discussions or participating in spiritual communities centered around sacred reading fosters a sense of community and connection, reducing feelings of isolation often experienced during the recovery process.

- **Holistic well-being:** Sacred reading contributes to holistic well-being by addressing the spiritual dimension of recovery, recognizing that the recovery journey involves not only physical and mental aspects but also spiritual and emotional dimensions.

- **Inspiration and motivation**: Sacred texts can inspire and motivate us by offering stories of resilience, transformation, and hope, serving as a source of encouragement on the path to recovery.

- **Personal growth:** The practice of sacred reading facilitates personal growth by encouraging us to explore and integrate the wisdom found in sacred texts into our lives, promoting a positive and transformative journey in recovery.

What are ways to practice sacred reading?

- **Religious scriptures:** Explore sacred texts from your own religious tradition, such as scriptures that hold spiritual significance for you.

- **Wisdom literature:** Read wisdom literature from various traditions, including philosophical writings that offer timeless insights and guidance.

- **Poetry:** Select spiritual or contemplative poetry that speaks to your soul and explores profound themes.

- **Mystical texts:** Delve into writings that emphasize a direct and experiential connection with the divine, exploring the mystical aspects of spirituality.

- **Mindfulness and meditation texts:** Choose texts that guide you in mindfulness and meditation practices, providing practical insights for your contemplative journey.

- **Self-help and inspirational literature:** Explore literature that aligns with your values and supports your journey in recovery, offering positive affirmations and practical guidance.

- **Ethical and moral teachings:** Study texts that focus on ethical and moral teachings, exploring virtues, compassion, and principles for leading a meaningful life.

- **Mind-body connection texts:** Explore writings that highlight the mind-body connection and the importance of holistic well-being, delving into the relationship between mental and physical health.

- **Philosophical texts:** Engage with philosophical texts that explore existential questions, the nature of existence, and the human experience, delving into profound philosophical reflections.

- **Daily devotionals:** Use daily devotionals that provide short readings and reflections for each day. These can offer a structured and focused approach to sacred reading.

Sacred reading can be a powerful tool in the recovery process, offering a holistic approach that addresses spiritual, emotional, and psychological aspects of our well-being. It's important to note that the effectiveness of sacred reading in recovery varies from person to person, and we may find different approaches that resonate with us. Additionally, incorporating sacred reading into a comprehensive recovery plan, alongside other therapeutic modalities and support systems, can enhance its positive impact.

"When walking, walk. When eating, eat."
— Zen proverb

MINDFUL MOVEMENT

What is the spiritual practice of mindful movement?

Mindful movement involves cultivating a heightened awareness and presence through intentional and conscious movement of the body. Rooted in mindfulness and often associated with traditions such as yoga, Tai Chi, and Qigong, this practice emphasizes the union of breath, body, and mind. Practitioners engage in slow, deliberate movements, paying close attention to the sensations, thoughts, and emotions arising in each moment. The aim is to foster a deep connection with the present, promoting a sense of inner calm and clarity. Mindful movement can be seen as a moving meditation, where we not only enhance our physical flexibility and strength but also cultivate a profound sense of mindfulness and spiritual well-being. This practice is not limited to specific religious traditions and is embraced by those seeking a holistic approach to spiritual growth and self-discovery.

How does mindful movement help recovery?

- **Stress reduction:** Mindful movement, through practices like yoga or Tai Chi, incorporates deep breathing and gentle, intentional motions. This can help reduce stress levels, which is crucial for those of us in recovery who may be dealing with heightened stress and anxiety.

- **Mind-body connection:** Mindful movement emphasizes the connection between the body and mind. This awareness promotes a better understanding of our physical sensations and emotional states, fostering a more integrated and balanced approach to recovery.

- **Emotional regulation:** Engaging in mindful movement provides a healthy outlet for processing and regulating emotions. It allows us to explore and release emotions in a constructive way, contributing to emotional well-being and resilience.

- **Improved self-awareness:** Mindful movement encourages self-reflection and increased awareness of thoughts and behaviors. This heightened self-awareness can be instrumental in identifying triggers, cravings, and other factors that may contribute to the challenges of recovery.

- **Enhanced focus and concentration:** The concentration required in mindful movement practices helps us develop better focus and concentration skills. This can be particularly helpful, as improved focus supports the development of coping strategies and decision-making abilities.

- **Building a routine:** Establishing a regular routine of mindful movement can contribute to a structured and healthy lifestyle. Consistency in practice reinforces positive habits and can replace harmful behaviors associated with addiction.

- **Community support:** Participating in group mindful movement classes or communities provides a sense of connection and support. Building positive social connections is vital for those of us in recovery, as it helps combat feelings of isolation.

- **Physical well-being:** Mindful movement contributes to physical health by improving flexibility, strength, and overall well-being. Physical health is interconnected with mental and emotional well-being, creating a holistic approach to recovery.

What are ways to practice mindful movement?

- **Yoga classes:** Attend yoga classes that focus on gentle movements, breath awareness, and meditation. Yoga helps recovery by fostering a sense of physical and emotional release, which is essential for healing.

- **Tai Chi sessions:** Join Tai Chi classes to experience the slow, flowing movements that promote balance and relaxation. Tai Chi reduces stress and provides a meditative focus that can replace addictive behaviors.

- **Qigong practices:** Explore Qigong exercises to enhance vitality and well-being through coordinated movements and breathwork. Qigong aids recovery by balancing the body's energy, reducing cravings, and enhancing mental clarity.

- **Walking meditation:** Practice walking meditation by paying attention to each step, breath, and the environment around you. This practice grounds us in the present moment, reducing anxiety and cravings.

- **Dance therapy classes:** Engage in dance therapy sessions to express emotions and promote self-discovery through movement. Dance therapy can facilitate emotional healing and provide a healthy outlet for the expression of feelings.

- **Mindful stretching:** Incorporate mindful awareness into stretching routines, focusing on each movement and breath. Mindful stretching helps by releasing muscle tension associated with stress and cravings, promoting relaxation.

- **Martial arts training:** Join martial arts classes to develop discipline, focus, and physical strength in a mindful way. Martial arts foster self-discipline and respect for oneself, which are crucial qualities for overcoming addiction.

- ✤ **Mindful breathing exercises:** Dedicate time to mindful breathing exercises, such as diaphragmatic breathing or box breathing. These exercises support recovery by helping to manage stress, reduce cravings, and improve emotional regulation.

- ✤ **Pilates workouts:** Include Pilates in your routine for core strength, flexibility, and body awareness. Pilates improves physical strength and self-esteem, which can be pivotal in overcoming addiction.

- ✤ **Gardening mindfully:** Engage in gardening activities with full awareness of each movement and the sensory experience. Mindful gardening nurtures a connection with nature and the present moment, offering therapeutic benefits and a sense of accomplishment that supports the recovery journey.

Mindful movement plays a significant role in supporting our recovery by addressing various aspects of our well-being, including stress management, emotional regulation, self-awareness, and the development of positive routines. These practices can be adapted based on your preferences, physical abilities, and accessibility. Combining different mindful movement activities or exploring what resonates best can contribute to a well-rounded approach to recovery. Consider consulting with healthcare professionals or instructors experienced in mindful movement for guidance and support.

"The child is in me still and sometimes not so still."
— Fred Rogers

SPIRITUAL HEALING APPLICATIONS

INNER CHILD

What is the spiritual application of the inner child?

The inner child refers to a psychological and spiritual perspective that views each of us as having an inner, childlike aspect within ourselves. This inner child represents the early experiences, emotions, and vulnerabilities that we carry from our childhood. It is often seen as the innocent, curious, and authentic self that can be overshadowed by the demands and conditioning of adulthood.

The inner child concept suggests that unresolved emotional wounds from childhood can continue to impact our thoughts, feelings, behaviors, and relationships in adulthood. Exploring and healing this inner child can lead to personal growth, emotional healing, and greater self-awareness. In a spiritual context, the inner child work involves reconnecting with and nurturing this aspect of ourselves through self-compassion, self-care, and inner healing practices. It aims to heal past wounds, release old patterns, and cultivate a sense of wholeness and authenticity. The inner child is seen as a source of creativity, intuition, and connection to a deeper sense of joy and vitality.

By acknowledging and integrating the inner child, we can experience spiritual and emotional transformation, leading to a more authentic and fulfilling life.

How does working with the inner child help recovery?

- **Recognizing unresolved trauma:** The inner child embodies the emotional imprints, unhealed wounds, and traumas of our formative years. Acknowledging and addressing these unresolved issues serve as fundamental steps toward healing and breaking the cycle of harmful behaviors.

- **Impact on present behavior:** Delving into the inner child's influence sheds light on how past traumas can shape current behaviors, including addictive tendencies. Such self-awareness paves the way for transformative change and growth.

- **Emotional expression:** The inner child carries unfiltered emotions that may have been stifled during times of addiction. Reconnecting with this aspect enables the safe and healthy expression of these emotions, fostering emotional balance.

- **Self-compassion:** Engaging with the inner child fosters a deep sense of self-compassion and self-care. This process mirrors the care we would provide to a child, nurturing the ability to treat oneself with kindness and empathy.

- **Healing and self-healing:** The inner child represents an avenue for personal healing. By addressing past wounds and offering the care and support needed, we embark on a journey of emotional healing and overall wellness.

- **Re-parenting:** Re-parenting the inner child involves providing ourselves with the care and attention that may have been absent during childhood. This practice empowers us to meet our emotional needs in positive and nurturing ways.

- **Reconnection with the authentic self:** Reconnecting with the inner child leads to rediscovering our authentic self, distinct from the facade created by addiction. This rediscovery fuels identity development and personal evolution.

- **Long-term recovery:** Integrating the inner child concept into the recovery process establishes a durable foundation for lasting healing. It equips us with tools to navigate challenges and construct a meaningful life in the realm of recovery.

What are ways to work on the inner child?

- **Identify core beliefs:** Reflect on the negative beliefs you hold about yourself that may have originated in childhood. These beliefs might be related to worthiness, love, or safety. Bringing these beliefs to light is the first step in challenging and changing them.

- **Set boundaries:** Establish healthy boundaries in your current relationships. Learning to say no and prioritize your needs helps you protect and care for your inner child.

- **Inner dialogue:** Engage in conversations with your inner child. Comfort and reassure them when you feel triggered or overwhelmed. Use compassionate and supportive language to address their fears and concerns.

- **Revisit old memories:** Explore your childhood memories with a compassionate and curious mindset. Try to understand your emotions and reactions during those times. This can provide insights into patterns and triggers that may still affect you.

- **Healing rituals:** Create rituals that symbolize your commitment to healing your inner child. Lighting a candle, writing affirmations, or even creating a physical space dedicated to your inner child can be powerful.

- **Emotional release:** Allow yourself to express suppressed emotions related to your childhood experiences. Cry, scream, or journal about your feelings. This can provide catharsis and help you release pent-up emotions.

- ✤ **Practice forgiveness:** Forgive yourself for any self-blame or guilt related to your past experiences. Also, consider forgiving those who may have hurt you, not for their sake but to release the emotional hold they have on you.

- ✤ **Therapeutic techniques:** Consider therapy modalities that specifically address inner child healing, such as inner child therapy, Gestalt therapy, or EMDR (Eye Movement Desensitization and Reprocessing).

- ✤ **Supportive community:** Connect with support groups, online forums, or communities focused on inner child healing and emotional well-being. Sharing your experiences and listening to others' stories can be validating and empowering.

- ✤ **Self-care:** Engage in activities that nourish your body, mind, and soul. Take regular breaks, engage in hobbies you enjoy, practice relaxation techniques, and prioritize your overall well-being.

Healing your inner child is a gradual and ongoing process. Be patient with yourself, and celebrate each step you take towards self-discovery and healing. If you find it challenging to navigate this journey on your own, seeking guidance from a qualified therapist or counselor can provide you with the necessary support and tools.

"She held herself until the sobs of the child inside subsided entirely. I love you, she told herself. It will all be okay." — H. Raven Rose

SELF-PARENTING

What is the spiritual application of self-parenting?

Self-parenting refers to the practice of taking on the role of a nurturing and supportive parent for oneself. It involves treating oneself with kindness, understanding, and compassion, similar to how a caring parent would treat their child. This concept is often used in the context of spiritual, emotional, and psychological well-being.

In self-parenting, we learn to provide ourselves with the emotional support and guidance we may not have received in our earlier years. This can include self-soothing techniques, setting boundaries, and making decisions that prioritize our own well-being. The goal is to develop a positive and nurturing inner dialogue, fostering self-love and resilience.

Practicing self-parenting can be especially beneficial for those of us who may have experienced a lack of emotional support or nurturing during our upbringing. It can contribute to improved mental health and a more positive self-image.

How can self-parenting help recovery?

- **Self-compassion:** Self-parenting encourages us to treat ourselves with kindness and understanding. It involves developing a compassionate inner dialogue, which can be particularly helpful in overcoming feelings of guilt or shame associated with addiction.

- **Setting boundaries:** Like a caring parent, those of us practicing self-parenting learn to set healthy boundaries. This involves recognizing and respecting one's own limits, saying no when necessary, and creating a supportive environment conducive to recovery.

- **Meeting emotional needs:** Self-parenting involves acknowledging and addressing one's emotional needs. Instead of relying solely on external sources for validation and support, we learn to self-soothe and provide emotional care for ourselves.

- **Self-care practices:** Just as a parent ensures the well-being of their child, self-parenting emphasizes the importance of self-care. This includes adopting healthy lifestyle habits, prioritizing physical and mental well-being, and engaging in activities that promote overall health.

- **Positive reinforcement:** Self-parenting involves recognizing and celebrating personal achievements and progress. This positive reinforcement can boost self-esteem and motivation, essential components of a successful recovery journey.

- **Inner guidance:** We often face challenging decisions in recovery. Self-parenting encourages the development of inner guidance and intuition, helping us make choices that align with our values and contribute to our well-being.

- **Responsibility and accountability:** Like a responsible parent, self-parenting involves taking responsibility for one's actions and choices. This includes being accountable for mistakes, learning from them, and making amends when necessary.

- **Cultivating a supportive inner voice:** Those of us practicing self-parenting work on cultivating an inner voice that is supportive and encouraging. This positive self-talk can counteract negative thought patterns that may hinder recovery.

What are ways to apply self-parenting?

🌿 **Practice Self-Compassion:** Speak to yourself with kindness and understanding. Replace self-criticism with supportive and encouraging self-talk.

🌿 **Set Healthy Boundaries:** Identify and communicate your personal limits to others. Learn to say no when necessary to protect your well-being.

🌿 **Meet Emotional Needs:** Acknowledge and validate your emotions without judgment. Engage in activities that bring emotional comfort and joy.

🌿 **Prioritize Self-Care:** Establish a routine that includes adequate sleep, nutrition, and exercise. Make time for activities that promote relaxation and stress reduction.

🌿 **Positive Reinforcement:** Celebrate your achievements, no matter how small. Focus on progress and growth rather than dwelling on setbacks.

🌿 **Inner Guidance:** Develop a sense of inner wisdom and intuition. Trust yourself to make decisions that align with your values.

🌿 **Responsibility and Accountability:** Take ownership of your actions and choices. Learn from mistakes and use them as opportunities for growth.

🌿 **Cultivate a Supportive Inner Voice***: Challenge negative self-talk with positive affirmations. Be your own source of encouragement during challenging times.

🌿 **Nurture Yourself:** Treat yourself with the same care and attention you would offer to a loved one. Prioritize activities that bring you joy and fulfillment.

- **Build a Supportive Network**: Surround yourself with positive influences. Seek support from friends, family, or a support group to reinforce your recovery journey.

Self-parenting is a personal and evolving process. It involves cultivating a nurturing relationship with yourself and actively participating in your own healing and growth.

Self-parenting in the context of recovery is about fostering self-compassion, self-care, and self-responsibility. It empowers us to take an active role in our healing journey and provides the internal support needed to navigate challenges and setbacks effectively.

"Once you replace negative thoughts with positive ones, you'll start having positive results."
— Willie Nelson

REFRAMING

What is the spiritual application of reframing?

Reframing involves changing how we perceive and interpret the events and narratives that have played significant roles in our lives. This approach encourages us to move from seeing life's challenges and our personal histories as barriers to recognizing them as catalysts for personal growth and enlightenment. Reframing allows for a mental and emotional shift, wherein past experiences are viewed not as sources of limitation but as opportunities for building resilience and empowerment. This shift does not alter the factual history of our lives but significantly changes how those facts impact our current and future emotional and psychological states.

Within the realms of self-help and spiritual development, reframing is often advocated as a powerful tool for breaking free from negative patterns or beliefs. It empowers us to re-examine our life stories, pinpointing and modifying those narratives that have held us back. The process is about more than just changing a story; it's about transforming our entire outlook on life, facilitating a journey from victimhood to a place of strength and purpose. By adopting this new perspective, we can enhance our mental well-being and pave the way for a life that is not only more satisfying but also more aligned with our deepest values and aspirations. Reframing is thus not a denial of the past but a strategic embrace of a new viewpoint, leading to greater spiritual health and a richer, more rewarding life experience.

How does reframing help recovery?

- **Empowerment:** Reframing empowers us by allowing us to take control of our narrative. It involves moving from a victim mindset to one of empowerment, where we recognize the capacity to shape our own story and recovery journey.

- **Positive perspective:** Reframing helps us adopt a more positive perspective on our past, present, and future. By focusing on strengths, resilience, and lessons learned, we can view challenges as opportunities for growth rather than insurmountable obstacles.

- **Reducing shame and guilt:** Many of us carry feelings of shame and guilt. Reframing allows us to address and release these negative emotions by understanding the context of our actions, acknowledging mistakes, and emphasizing the progress made in recovery.

- **Identity transformation:** Reframing facilitates a transformation of self-identity. Instead of being defined solely by past mistakes or struggles, we can redefine ourselves in terms of our strengths, values, and aspirations.

- **Motivation for change:** Reframing provides motivation for change by illustrating the positive outcomes that can emerge from the recovery journey. It helps us envision a future filled with purpose, connection, and personal fulfillment.

- **Strengthening relationships:** Reframing can positively impact relationships. As we develop a more compassionate and understanding view of ourselves, we are often better equipped to build and maintain healthy connections with others.

- **Preventing relapse:** By reframing negative thought patterns and promoting a positive mindset, we can reduce the risk of relapse. This shift in perspective contributes to a more sustainable and resilient recovery process.

- **Spiritual growth:** For those with a spiritual orientation, reframing can align with spiritual beliefs, fostering a sense of purpose, connection, and transcendence on the recovery journey.

What are ways to reframe?

- **From victim to survivor:** Reframe yourself as a survivor rather than a victim, emphasizing strength and resilience. This perspective honors your journey and the obstacles you've overcome, highlighting your power and determination.

- **Learning opportunities:** View challenges as opportunities for learning and personal development. Each challenge is a stepping stone towards becoming more skilled and adaptable.

- **Embracing imperfection:** Shift from a focus on perfection to embracing imperfection, understanding that it's okay not to be perfect. This acceptance fosters a healthier self-image and reduces unnecessary stress and anxiety.

- **Strength in vulnerability:** See vulnerability as a strength rather than a weakness, fostering authentic connections with others. It invites deeper relationships and builds trust, showing that true strength includes openness and emotional honesty.

- **Self-compassion:** Replace self-judgment with self-compassion, treating yourself with the same kindness you would a friend. This approach nurtures inner peace and promotes a more positive and forgiving self-relationship.

- **Resilience in setbacks:** Instead of seeing setbacks as failures, view them as opportunities to build resilience and learn from the experience. Each setback teaches valuable lessons, contributing to your growth and strength.

- ৶ **Reframing mistakes:** See mistakes as opportunities for growth and learning rather than as evidence of personal failure. This mindset encourages continuous improvement and a healthy acceptance of the learning process.

- ৶ **Creating a new narrative:** Rewrite your story, emphasizing the positive changes and transformations you've experienced. This new narrative celebrates your evolution and the journey towards a more fulfilling life.

- ৶ **Identity beyond addiction:** Explore and redefine your identity beyond the constraints of addiction. Discovering new hobbies, interests, and values contributes to a fuller sense of self and a more rewarding life.

- ৶ **Empowerment narrative:** Craft a narrative that emphasizes your ability to take control and make positive choices in your recovery journey. This story reinforces your agency and capability, inspiring continued progress and empowerment.

Reframing can be a powerful and therapeutic tool in the process of recovery by changing how we perceive and interpret our life experiences. It encourages resilience, promotes a positive self-image, and helps us move away from negative patterns. Embracing imperfections, learning from setbacks, and treating ourselves with compassion are key aspects of this mindset shift. Reframing is a continuous process that involves consciously choosing a narrative that supports healing, growth, and positive change. It provides a framework for us to navigate challenges, build resilience, and cultivate a more hopeful and optimistic outlook on our recovery journey.

CONCLUSION

As you journey forward, keep in mind that the paths of recovery and spiritual awakening are not linear journeys but spirals of continual growth and expansion. The insights and practices shared within these pages are not meant to be destinations but signposts marking the way toward a richer, more vibrant existence. The role of spirituality in the realm of recovery is profound, offering more than mere solutions to challenges—it infuses life with a deeper sense of purpose, interconnectedness, and tranquility.

Spirituality + Recovery: A Practical Guide to Spiritual Concepts, Principles and Practices used in Recovery and the Twelve Steps has extended an invitation for you to embark on a transformative journey, blending spirituality and recovery to nurture a state of wellness, meaning, and limitless possibility. As you continue along this path, may this book serve as a steadfast companion, a light guiding you back to the immense power that resides within, and a map that leads you to the rediscovery of your own inner haven of peace, strength, and wisdom.

In conclusion, remember that the journey does not end with the final page of this guide. Each day presents new opportunities for growth, healing, and self-discovery. May your journey be illuminated by the enduring power of spiritual growth, and may it be graced with light, love, and infinite possibilities.